A Civil Servant

My Life With Bureaucracy

Morton A Lebow

A CIVIL SERVANT Copyright © 2018 by Morton Lebow

All rights reserved no part of this book may be reproduced or transmitted in any form or by any means electronic or mechanical without permission in writing from the copyright owner.

Library of Congress Control Number 1-6651435321

Acknowledgments

I must thank Art Dagamengian whose curiosity changed our lives for the better. The friendships I encountered at Social Security with Charlie Miller, Ray Lannon and Joe Preissig lasted throughout my career. Each one was not only a friend but without their influence my career would have taken a different and not so rewarding path.

The men who I would call my bosses not only encouraged me but by their examples demonstrated what it meant to be good public servants. Hink Porter at Social Security, Bob Hutchings at the water pollution control program, Stew Hunter at the Surgeon General's office and Ken Endicott at the Health Manpower program all were not only good friends but also great mentors. And a special thanks to Malcolm Forsythe who made it possible for us to explore Kent and the British National Health Service

Michael Wangler, the Nobel Laureate, who deciphered the internet for me so that this book could come into being in its present form deserves special mention. As does Florence Foelak who for the 20 years we worked together meant so much to whatever success I had by making sure any of my wild ideas successfully came to fruition.

And finally, my wife, Eileen who not only lived through the many changes in our lives but carved out her very successful careers as a teacher and published author.

A Civil Servant

George Richards was a claims representative at the Social Security office in Rochester, NY. During the depths of the depression, George worked as a milk salesman to make a living and had to endure the depressing experience of standing in a line once a week with the other salesmen to explain to the boss, when he did not make his quota of sales, why he had failed.

When a job became available during the early days of the Social Security program he leapt at the opportunity, not only to get rid of the albatross that his salesman's job had become, but to work in an environment where he could actually help people.

Over the years, George developed a method of dealing with people who came to apply for old age or survivors' payments. He would unsmilingly call the applicant by name holding the file on which was clearly marked the person's name, age and social security number. Then, still unsmiling, and often frowning for effect, he would lead the claimant or claimants in the case of a married couple to an interview table where they sat facing each other. He then would ask the person for his or her social security card: completely unneeded since already had the number in the file.

When the person handed him the card, George's demeanor changed immediately. He smiled and said with great enthusiasm, "Mr. DeAngelo, do you know that this is one of the first cards ever issued!" (He didn't mention that it was along with about 20 million others) Suddenly, the whole tenor of the transaction changed. The claimant was now a person of some importance. By the time the interview was finished, they were friends and often walked to the exit with their arms around each other.

Chapter One

Come One, Come All

Summer 1950

I was in the process of finishing up the box office chores as the season ran down when I received the letter forwarded by my mother from the Civil Service Commission asking me to report to the New York regional office for a job interview. Since I was in no hurry to leave Cape Cod for any government job, I replied that I would be back in New York after Labor Day and would then get in touch with them. I wasn't about to miss the last show of the season at the Hyannis Music Circus.

It had been a hugely successful season after a slow start. After papering the house with groups from retirement homes and children's camps for the first two shows, the matinee of the third show "Naughty Marietta" was sold out. When word spread of the sold out show, the demand for tickets increased almost overnight.

The early rehearsals for "Showboat" weren't going too well, so the management recruited the director Bobby Jarvis to liven things up. He put out a call to the staff of the theater asking for anyone who wanted to play a short role. Since the work at the box office had slacked off with few tickets available, I decided to take a shot at being a thespian.

The Hyannis Music Circus was a tent show in the round; one of three Cape Cod theaters operated by Richard Aldrich which included the Mashpee Playhouse and the famed Cape Playhouse. There were four aisles that led down to the stage, so Jarvis asked the fledgling actors to play the parts of barkers at the sideshows on the midway at the Chicago World's Fair at the opening of the second act. I asked Jarvis what I should say and was told to make up any old patter as long as it was loud. All I had to do, as the lights went out was to step into the spotlight at the top of the aisle and deliver my spiel until the spotlight faded.

And that's what I did, decked out in a multi-colored jacket with a straw hat and a cane, I spouted "Come one. Come all. See Sheba the Queen of them all. For one thin dime you can see the beauty that captured minds of crowds in the Orient. She shakes and shimmies. For one thin dime.

All went well for the first two performances. Then as I was finishing spiel for the Wednesday matinee with "She shakes and shimmies" the audience around me broke out in laughter as I noticed too late that a rather rotund woman was hurrying to her seat. Four days later my theater career came to an end, and I hurried back to New York for the job interview that was waiting for me.

I really didn't know what I wanted to do with the rest of my life, but a job in the government would do until something better came along. I took the subway down to 40 Broadway where I was met with a government official who explained that because of the recent changes to the Social Security Act, they expected the need for people to handle the increased workload. I was then offered a list of job openings both in New York City as well as upstate New York.

Feeling it was time to get away from the city, I picked an opening in Rochester on Lake Ontario and prepared for the change in my life. But before I had to leave the City, I had to meet Eileen, the woman who would later become my wife, as she returned from California. We would have three days together, before I had to drive upstate.

After I saw her settled in her job and new apartment, we parted and I drove the 325 miles to my new life with the promise to stay in touch.

Chapter Two

Call It Americanism

1950-1955

The Social Security office in Rochester was a long rather narrow one with the reception area blocked off with a three foot railing behind which the receptionists took down the relevant information like name, date of birth and social security number and collected any other documents the claimant needed. On the left side as you walked away were the claims representatives desks, and on the right were the tables at which the claims interviews took place.

I was assigned to Mamie Burleigh, an experienced claims rep with a soft Southern accent betraying her Georgia roots who would oversee my work as I learned my job and who became a longtime friend. At the next desk was George Richards who, it seems, was unofficially designated to take the new hires in hand and tell them what it was like to work for the Social Security

Administration. He would make it a point to go to lunch with me and the other new ones and tell us what it was like working as a milk salesman during the height of the depression having to line up once a week to report on why they had not met their sales goal if they hadn't. "And here," he would say with a great deal of pride, "you can really make life better for the people you serve." And he really meant it.

I would watch him greet the nervous applicants knowing that after the receptionist handed George a folder, he would walk grimly to the reception area and, still unsmiling, go through his routine of turning the anxious and often nervous client into a relaxed and good friend.

The work was fairly interesting as I learned the intricacies involved with taking claims from people who were retiring or from the widows of workers who had passed away. And I saw, with mounting annoyance, the funeral directors who often accompanied the bereaved. I already learned from reviewing the bills from the undertakers that the funeral directors, especially those who served the large Italian community, were preying on the surviving family members to purchase unnecessary and expensive services that inflated the bills from families who were often not flushed with cash. But I was a little helpless knowing that it would be inappropriate to interfere with the relationships between the surviving families and the funeral directors who were often close members of the same communities, but oh I wished I could.

Aside from the day to day work at the office, the people working there were a congenial and dedicated group. I became friendly with many of them including Pete Soppas who had preceded me as a trainee by about six months. It was a friendship that would ultimately and abruptly greatly change the course of my life several years later. We formed a close bond of friendship on the handball court of the YMCA where we both lived and the frequent week-end tips to and from New York and Rochester.

For much of the seven months I was in training I would make the 325 mile drive to New York to spend the week-ends with Eileen until finally she came to live and work in Rochester for the then thriving Eastman Kodak company. We both enjoyed the company of the friends I had made at the office and we especially enjoyed our own closeness exploring the beauties of upper state New York.

Pete had been promoted to Field Representative in the Geneva, NY social security office, and when Eileen and I set the date for our simple wedding, Pete came up to witness the brief and private ceremony.

Then, just short of a year in Rochester, I was offered a promotion to be a Field Representative at the office in Sunbury, Pennsylvania. Sunbury with a population of about 17,000, was the county seat of Northumberland County perched on the west bank of the Susquehanna River just where it divided going North toward New York and East toward the hard coal region of Pennsylvania. The job would involve meeting with claimants at locations in the coal regions to the East and the farming area across the river on the western side of the river.

After finding an apartment and settling in, I took leave and hurried back to Rochester for the intimate marriage ceremony with Eileen and a brief honeymoon at Niagara Falls and Canada. After one night on the U.S. side, we crossed the border agreeing that any newly married couple was too easily identified at that honeymoon venue on the New York side. After looking around on the Canadian side, we took the elevator to the restaurant at the top of the Hotel General Brock for a memorable meal of oysters that would live in our memories as the best oysters we had ever eaten until we returned again sixty years later. The view looking down at the falls from their perch atop the hotel was a breathtaking one.

After another night on the Canadian side we returned to the United States and south to our new life together in Sunbury. Eileen, with her excellent typing skills and extremely good looks, had no trouble getting a job. I meanwhile began to get familiar with my new routine. Once a month, I would travel over the river to Selinsgrove where I would set up office for the day.

The other time was devoted to the more populous area in the anthracite coal country. Two days a week, I set up my office in the unemployment office in Shamokin. On the other days I visited people in their homes when they could not make it into the office.

The office in Sunbury, was on the second floor of a commercial building near the square. In addition to me, the office was staffed by a manager, Drexel Winner, a receptionist and two claims representatives; one of whom, Jim Sullivan, was a trainee who I helped get prepared for his promotion to a full-fledged claims representative. He would become a lifelong friend. Drexel was an addicted smoker who, when I was away from the office, would sit at my desk. When I returned, I would count the cigarette butts and tell how long he had been there--15 minutes per butt. One day I returned to an ashtray heaped high with butts. When I looked up, the entire office, each one of whom had contributed, was laughing.

It was in this office, one day that a modestly dressed woman came to file a survivor's claim. Her husband of more than 20 years had just died, and she was there to get benefits for herself and her two minor children. As with so many recent widows, she carried with her an air of sadness. She produced the death certificate and her children's birth certificates. When I asked for her marriage certificate to complete the claim, she became a little embarrassed and, looking down, muttered, "We were a common law marriage. You see, when we wanted to get married, his first wife was still around."

I tried at her to put her at ease, "That's OK, Pennsylvania recognizes common law marriages."

I wrote out a statement for her to sign. She left the office much relieved. And I felt pretty good until about ten days later when I got notice that her claim was denied, because when she entered into the common law union with her now deceased husband, his legally married wife cancelled out the common law arrangement. I was stunned and wondered what would George Richards do in a case like this. After mulling over the options, I decided to call the widow in and try to work out some solution.

It was a few days later, when she arrived. As we sat at my desk, I knew that the rest of the office was watching to see how I was going to resolve the problem. There was no way to get around it, so I plunged in.

"Mrs. Wagner, the claim we submitted was turned down..."

Before I could continue, I saw the look of terror in her eyes

"But!!..."

I held up my hand to try to calm her down and rushed to say, "Let me ask you something. Did your husband's first wife die while you were both together?"

Still with that look of bewilderment, she nodded.

Trying to act as reassuring as I could, "Now, when she died, did your husband say, 'Now we can be married legally?'"

She nodded and then with some hesitation, in a low voice, said, "Yes."

"Good, so, in effect, you had a new agreement. Now let's write out a statement for you, and we'll see if that can fix this up."

And that's what we did. It was just a week later that the claim was approved. I had to admit that I was relieved and thought "George would have approved." It was moments like this that made me feel that I was doing something useful.

About once a week, I would invite Jim Sullivan to join me and go home for some of Eileen's home cooked meals. We would leave the office and usually were blocked as a slow moving freight train of about 100 cars lumbered through the town. Although we would always stick to the claim that we didn't plan it that way, we would always stop for a beer at the bar alongside the train tracks. By the time the train had passed, we had finished our beers and were ready for dinner with Eileen.

Jim would soon give up social security and even though he moved away to become a foreign service courier, we would stay in touch for the rest of his life.

And this was pretty much our routine during the week. On weekends, Sunbury became a very busy market town with the farmers coming over from the west side of the river to shop and gawk at the shops and the people on Main Street.

It was on the two days that I covered the anthracite region that became the most interesting. It was the beginning of the long period where the hard coal industry was sliding toward its final days. Many of my days, would be spent visiting retired miners, often ill and suffering from silicosis which they had contracted from their long work underground in the mines. I would chat with them about what it was like down there in the dark with only the light from their helmets to break the darkness.

Before I talked to them, I had assumed, the city boy that I was, that they would be happy to be away from their underground existence. But very quickly I found that I was so wrong when taking a claim from Claus Werner who sat in an armchair connected to an oxygen tank. Mr. Werner had worked in a defense plant in Philadelphia during the war.

"It was working by the bells." he said while breathing in his oxygen. "You would start to work when the bells rang, and stopped when they rang again."

"But wasn't it better than working down there in the mines?"

Werner shook his head, "Naw! Down there, you're on your own. If you get hungry, you stop and take out the sandwich the Mrs. got up for me and eat it. There were no bells telling you what you could do or what you couldn't do. No, working down there, you were your own boss."

I still couldn't understand it. Here, this man was dying of silicosis he got working in the darkness of a coal mine, but that was the life he knew and liked, because down there underground, he felt he was his own boss. Then, when I finished with the paperwork for the claim, I rose to go, and Mr. Werner, still breathing through his oxygen mask, said, "Thanks a lot for coming by."

It was a routine that was repeated over and over again during my year as a field representative out of the Sunbury office.

With the presidential election coming up, Eileen and I trotted down to the county election office to register to vote. When asked how long we had lived in Pennsylvania, we told the clerk we had moved there last October and were startled to hear the clerk tell us that would not be long enough since you had to be residents by the end of registration which was September. We had missed being residents by one month. We argued that we would have been there a year by election time in November to no avail.

When we got home, I decided to call the Republican county chairman to explain our case and was pleasantly surprised to hear him say, "Go back and tell Helen to register you. I'll give her a call. Which is what we did and registered as Republicans in that very Republican county.

After the Republican convention when General Eisenhower was nominated, a giant photograph of him was hung in one of the two courthouse towers facing the main square. It was after the Democratic convention when another picture of Eisenhower was displayed on the other tower. Since I, as a federal employee, could not engage in politics, Eileen wrote a letter to the local newspaper, *The Sunbury Item* stating that "as a registered Republican, I am shocked by the partisanship displayed by the county officials in not putting up a picture of Adlai Stevenson."

The Republican county officials responded by putting up Stevenson's picture on the side of the front tower facing the alley where few people would see it. A short time later, President Harry Truman came through on a whistle stop trip for Adlai Stevenson. One of his stops was in Northumberland, just across the river north of

Sunbury. I closed up shop in Shamokin and drove back to pick up Eileen. As the President began to talk, a number of people in the crowd began heckling. One of them was standing next to us. Eileen turned to berate him and said, "I came to hear the president!"

"Lady, you're not gonna hear much today."

Whereupon Eileen let him have it. "What did you do, hire a bunch of thugs to come out and shout?"

Then Eileen wrote another classic letter to the editors which appeared the next day.

One of the duties I had as a field representative was to track down employers who had omitted reporting their workers social security numbers. It was on one of those trips that I received a real shock. I drove south from Sunbury along the river looking for a chicken farm which I finally found and was astonished to see a rabbi supervising the slaughter of chickens. A rabbi here in the middle of Dutch Pennsylvania!

I remember asking the owner, "What is the rabbi doing here in the middle of this area?"

Answering with a smile, the boss said, "You see, we moved here from Brooklyn a few years ago. Labor costs are much lower here, but our buyers want kosher stuff to sell back in Brooklyn. We truck the kosher chickens into Brooklyn three or four times a week, and everyone is happy."

The longer I worked in this area in the middle of the state, the more I was impressed with the difference 25 miles was making. In Sunbury, the county seat, you found a staid, market town that served a conservative farming population that had lived in the area for generations, but a mere 25 miles to the east in Shamokin, the vibrant population was mainly Eastern European who were only first or second generation Americans.

I shared my thoughts with Eileen, so we drove over to Shamokin one Saturday to show her this different world, and where we discovered a great ice cream store. How different from calm world of Sunbury.

On weekends, we would often attend the farm auctions for entertainment and to see if, on our limited budget, we could buy a thing or two. By now, Eileen was pregnant expecting our first child, so it was much to our surprise when we saw the auctioneer hold up a shabbily grey painted cradle. And also, much to our surprise, we had it for $2.50.

When I mentioned our prize in the office the following Monday, John, one of the claims reps, volunteered that he would like to see it. After work, we stopped at the house. John examined the cradle and nodded.

"Hmm. It's an old one. Probably made before 1825."

"How to you know?"

"Well, these are hand wrought nails. And they pretty much went out of style after 1825 when machine nails were invented."

Thereafter, with John's guidance, I spent my spare time removing the dirty grey paint and was so pleasantly surprised to find that it was a handsome handmade walnut cradle. With the small mattress I had made to order, the cradle was ready for our newly born daughter, Ellen.

But the weekend farm auctions had gotten under our skins, and we began accumulating a few handmade pieces of furniture for our home--a handmade double bed, a couple of Dutch farm kitchen sinks, a broken down chest of drawers which I would later refinish to find it was walnut with curly maple drawers.

When Eileen gave birth to Ellen. The local doctor induced the birth since he told us, he couldn't be sure that he would be available if the birth proceeded naturally. Everything was fine for a few days, and then Eileen began bleeding and had to go back to the hospital. It was a tense moment for both of us, but eventually everything sorted itself out.

Finally, after 18 months there on the banks of the Susquehanna River, it was time to move on, and I was offered the chance to run the one man station in Chambersburg, about 50 miles west of my soon to be parent office in Harrisburg. There in the college town that had been the scene of a Civil War engagement as a prelude to the battle of Gettysburg, we settled in for another year and the birth of our second child--a son. Once again, Eileen had to rush to the hospital for a caesarian birth, and Ellen had a baby brother, Edward.

The office in Chambersburg was a two room affair on the second floor of a small office building on the same floor with the town's radio station. One room was the waiting area, the other was where I would conduct the business of taking claims. My territory covered two counties. I held office hours two days a week in Chambersburg and one day a week in the employment office in McConnellsburg about 20 miles to the west.

I spent some time and made friends with the personnel at the radio station, and, after a few months, I made a proposition that they give me 15 minutes each week to give the public information about social security and answer any questions listeners might have. I quickly found a receptive listening audience, but when I approached the local newspaper to ask them to list my program, I discovered a rivalry between the print and broadcast media with the newspaper's reluctance to give any space to what they viewed as their competitor.

Not willing to accept this as the final answer, I offered the newspaper a weekly column with social security information. The editor snapped up the idea of a free column, and I not only had my 15 minutes on the air, but also a weekly social security column which I was able to keep up with releases that the central office in Baltimore provided.

In my wanderings around the countryside, I came upon a bearded Mr. Wingert, an Amish farmer who, with his wife, his 16 year old son and 18 year old daughter ran a farm of some hundred acres. He was a River Brethren who, among other things, believed in baptism in the flowing stream. There was no mechanism on the farm as he explain to me one day, "God, put the beast of burden on this earth to serve man."

But what the farm did offer was an array of farm products including the best home cured bacon slabs that Eileen and I ever had. One day when I stopped by the make a purchase, Mr. Wingert and I were chatting while waiting for the bacon to be wrapped up. It was during the height of the McCarthy period, and although the farmer had no radio, he was very much aware of what was going on in the political world.

"You know" he said while leaning on the fence, "they talk about all those isms: communism, fascism..." I thought I knew what was coming, but was unprepared for the next line which i would carry with me for the rest of my life.

"When it comes here, we're gonna call it Americanism!"

Although we had settled in to that lovely town and had made many good friends in Chambersburg, another change loomed. I was offered the assistant manager's post at Lancaster, Pennsylvania. It was too good an opportunity to turn down, so another move came into our lives.

Lancaster was quite a contrast with Chambersburg. A city of about 50,000, it served a two county area with the Amish and Mennonite population to the East near towns with such romantic names as Intercourse and Paradise and North with the larger city of Lebanon. The territory extended West to the Susquehanna River and the town of Columbia.

The manager of the office, Muncie Gleaton, had been there for some time and had a farm across the river where he raised a number of crops including some of the best corn that we ever ate. And he never let us go out to harvest the corn until the water was boiling in the pot.

It was a busy office, and shortly after I arrived to take up my duties, the office was flooded with a stream of applicants because of a change in the law. Seeing the reception area becoming crowded and the staff working furiously, I began taking claims and even pressed Muncie into doing the same to relieve some of the pressure on the claims reps.

From time to time, I noticed a group of Amish women coming in together to file claims and asked one of the claims reps what was going on. She explained, "They had suspended their widows' benefits, and now they want to get them started again."

"But why did they suspend them?"

"A new Bishop came in and told them that the community would take care of them. After a while. the Bishop leaves, and they can't get by on what the community gives them, so they come in again."

Grant Means, one of the claims reps, had a father who was a chef at Lancaster's best hotel, so from time to time, Grant, Muncie and I would go down and feast on the special mock turtle soup laced with the sherry that was served. Between those lunches, and visits to Lebanon and Columbia to help take care of business at those locations, I became quite comfortable in helping run the busy office.

One day, there was a notice in the local newspaper that Miss Evelyn Aye, Miss America that year from Ephrata which was in the northern part of our territory was going to be married. Thinking it might be a good idea to get publicity for our program, I got in touch with her and asked if she would be willing to publicize the fact that she was changing her name on her social security card. To my pleasant surprise, she readily agreed and a date was set for her to come to the office and pose for photographs.

She visited the office and graciously posed for a photo as she signed the change of name form. I composed a news release, which would not pass muster years later as the feminist movement gathered steam.

"Miss America, Evelyn Aye, today did what every woman about to be married should do. "

Then I sent it off to the public information office at headquarters in Baltimore, Maryland feeling quite good about the whole thing.

About a month later, the decision was made to move the office from its present location in downtown out to a location where parking would become available. In planning the move, remembering how well it worked in Rochester, I thought that instead of keeping the practice of taking the claims at the cluttered claims reps' desks, it would be a good idea to use separate interview tables.

Some of the people in the office didn't like the idea of having to get up from their desks to meet the claimants. I finally convinced them that in addition to getting a little exercise, it would be more pleasant for the visitors to the office , and interview desks were installed.

From time to time, there were notices of positions in the Baltimore office that were available. There was one that particularly interested me. It was a newly created position to work with groups and organizations to help explain social security. It looked as if it would be interesting. After talking it over with Eileen, I decided to apply for the job. I did and heard nothing thinking that they had hired someone else for the job.

Shortly after that, I received a visit from the Assistant Regional Representative from the New York office who offered me the job of Manager of the New Castle office in Western Pennsylvania. I, of course, accepted the office and thought nothing of the requirement that I agree to stay there for at least one year.

So another move was in the works.

Muncie and his wife agreed to mind the two kids on their farm near Wrightsville while Eileen and I scouted living quarters in New Castle. We drove across the state and after a day or two were able to locate a house on a pleasant street in New Castle that was just a five minute drive to the office, and the move was set.

The New Castle office was much like the one in Sunbury with a fairly small staff and covering a two county area north of Pittsburgh. the town was in the process of slipping into a mild depression as the major industry, a giant tool plant, was closing and moving elsewhere. The office pretty much ran itself, but on an occasion or two each month, I would travel over to Butler to take claims in a national guard armory.

It was there that I became friendly with the Captain, who was in charge of that national guard unit. After a few months, he approached me with an offer I easily and immediately refused. He offered me a commission in the national guard, but I laughed and said, "Look, I served my time in the infantry in France in one war, and that's enough for me."

After about a month in New Castle, I received an order from the Regional office in New York, that we should work on the following Saturday to clear up any work we had hanging over us before the end of the fiscal year. I checked with the two claims reps and found that there was actually little work to catch up on, so I notified the region that there was no need for us to come in on Saturday.

I was quickly informed that the Saturday work day was an order since the region had funds that would be returned if they were not used by the end of the fiscal year. So bowing to the whims of bureaucracy, we came in on Saturday.

Then, the peaceful routine in New Castle was upended. A letter came from our Rochester friend, Pete Soppas who was now in the central office in

Baltimore. A fellow named Art Dagamengian was going through some reading files and came across one with my name, and he asked Pete if he knew me. Apparently, the Public Information Office had been interested in interviewing me for the job working with groups and organizations, but the Regional Representative, Bob Fraker had sent a memo without bringing me on board telling them that I was not available. And Pete thought that I might want to know.

Now I knew why I had been asked to commit to a year in New Castle. I also knew what I was going to do. Although we had settled nicely in New Castle, I was offended that the decision about my career had been made without consulting me.

I sat down and composed a letter to the regional office saying that I would be interested in several jobs that had been advertised in the central office but was most interested in the one in the Public Information Office for which they had turned me down without consulting me.

The response was immediate. I received a call from the Assistant Regional Rep who said, with a hint of a smile, "Bob Fraker would like to chat with

31

you before the meeting here at the regional office starts"

I answered, also with a hint of a smile, "I thought he would."

When I met with Fraker in New York, he explained that with the budget constraints, they wanted to make sure their offices were staffed with the best people they had. I was having none of this.

"Look Bob, whenever you wanted me and my family to move, we did even though many times it meant no immediate raise in pay or grade, I was always willing to do it, and we've enjoyed wherever we were, but to turn me down with this opportunity without even talking to me doesn't seem fair."

And it was agreed that Fraker would notify central office that I was, indeed available for an interview if the position was still available. And it was.

Within a week, I was told to travel to Baltimore for a job interview. It was there that I met Hinkley Porter who would be my supervisor. I had a chance to see Pete Soppas and meet for the first time my benefactor, Art Dagamenjian whom I thanked profusely. A date was set, and I was prepared to give up my short lived post in New Castle for a new career as the person who would work with groups and organizations to spread the word about how social security would affect their members.

Chapter Three

Bill Davis Gets A Social Security Card

1955-1962

The first thing we had to do before reporting for the job was to find a place to live, and we were lucky finding a first floor apartment in a pleasant section of Baltimore within easy walking distance of the streetcar that would take me to work downtown. Since we didn't have too much furniture, the move was fairly painless.

Hink Porter, my new boss, explained on the first day that the position was a brand new one, so I was going to have to define the job as I went along with him looking over my shoulders. I was going to have to match the national organizations to the needs of the program.

The public information staff wasn't that large for the job they had to do of explaining the social security program to the whole country. Wallace

Kendall was in charge of the media section with two talented people, Charlotte Crenson, the press officer, and Broughton Tall, the writer. Aside from Hink, there was Walt Rosenberg and me. Roy Swift, a transplanted Texan, was in charge of the whole operation.

It took me a week or two to comprehend what I was going to do, but with Hink guiding me, I gradually began to form some idea of how I was going to go about it. I began to match the requirements of the law with the groups that might benefit from it and then try to find out what organizations represented those people who needed information about how they might benefit from the law.

Shortly after I arrived in Baltimore, the law was extended to cover migrant farm workers, but if I was going to get usable information to those workers, I knew, the city boy that I was, that I had to understand the conditions under which they worked, so with a fellow from the field operations unit, we set up a schedule of visits to migrant worker camps on the Eastern Shore of Maryland and later in the apple orchards of the Shenandoah Valley of Virginia and West Virginia.

And it was a real education for this city boy from New York.

We drove down from Baltimore on a brief tour of the migrant labor camps in the farming areas in Southern Maryland and the Northern neck of Virginia. Seeing for the first time the living conditions under which the imported workers mainly from the Florida orchards were living.

At each camp, we first had to check in with the camp manager who had a fairly comfortable but Spartan house at the entrance to the farm. In chatting with the manager, I noted the rifle rack near on the wall and asked, "Do you ever have to use that?"pointing to the guns.

"Yeah" he responded, "but not too often. As long as they know it's there, they don't wanna cause any trouble."

After getting permission from the manager, we went out into the field to seek out the crew leaders--the ones who took in the money from the camp manager and distributed the remains, after taking their fee, to the workers in their crews. I was beginning to see how difficult it was going to be to get social security information passed on to the workers.

It was a routine that was repeated with only minor variations at each of the three camps we visited before we returned to Baltimore. I discussed our findings with Hink and confessed that it wasn't going to easy to get information to the field workers but was encouraged to keep at it.

So, after a week or two at headquarters, we headed toward the apple orchards of the Shenandoah Valley and a very different environment. Although the general outlines of what we had found previously prevailed there, the setup seemed much more organized. When we spoke to the crew leaders, there seemed to be a much closer relationship between the leaders and the men they supervised. It seemed almost like an extended family.

We had arrived there toward the end of the picking season, but I noticed that many trees still had apples on them. I pointed this out to one crew leader and asked, "How come you left those apples on the trees?"

The crew leader smiled and told me "those were all touched with the frost and won't last until they got in the stores. We only pick the ones that will still be good by the time they're in the store."

Then he asked, "Do you want some? They're still good."

Of course, I agreed, and the crew leader picked a batch for me and dumped them in the trunk of my car saying, "I'll keep the crate." And when I brought them home, Eileen and I both agreed they were some of the sweetest apples we ever tasted.

But I was still faced with the problem of how to get information about social security to the farm workers. I began looking for any organizations that worked with these people. It was then that I discovered a group called the Migrant Ministry of the National Council of Churches. Although they worked out of New York, they had a Washington office. It was there speaking with the two women who ran the Ministry that I came up with part of the answer.

Monica Owens, one of the two, said, "You know, we run literacy classes in the camps. If you could get us easy to read material, we would certainly be willing to use it in our classes."

It was an idea that was to have far reaching effect that I brought back to the office. I discussed the idea with Hink and Roy Swift, At first Roy wasn't thrilled with the idea of "dumbing down" social security information, but I pressed the idea.

"Why don't we at least try it on a trial basis, and see how it works out?"

And it was agreed that Mr. Tall, working with me would develop a reading lesson that the Migrant Ministry could use. No one at that moment even had any idea of what this experiment would lead to.

Mr. Tall then produced a pamphlet entitled "Bill Davis Gets A Social Security Card." It was illustrated and used very simple language. When I showed the prototype to Monica, she asked for 5,000 copies, and the experiment was on its way with a bang.

Suddenly, out of nowhere, the office was inundated with requests for this "dumbed down" version. Then I realized that some of the requests were coming from unlikely sources like the Adult Education Department in New York City--hardly a dense farming area. I phoned the woman who had made the call. After identifying myself, I pointed out that the reading lesson was really designed for farm workers and not city dwellers.

"O.K." she replied, "but it's the first literacy material that's dealing with an adult subject matter."

I must have sounded like a dimwit "I don't understand"

She then pointed out to me that practically all literacy material was of the "See spot run" variety, and they would gladly use this material."

"What if we produced one that could be used by anyone like people in the cities!"

And that's what we did, and we were inundated with requests from literacy programs in all parts of the country. I had my first best seller. I also had an introduction to the needs of the large adult population who could only read at a very low level. It was an idea that stayed with me for my whole career. "How can you reach hard to reach groups?"

A short time later, I ran into a slight problem. The social security law allowed veterans to credit their time on active duty toward calculating their social security benefits. It was a provision that hadn't been widely publicized, so I decided to get in touch with the national veteran's organization and see how they could spread the word.

The largest one and the one I first called on was the American Legion at their headquarters in Washington. I called to set up an appointment and scheduled a visit for the following week. When I met with the Legion's representative, I could tell that they weren't going to fall over themselves listening to another government bureaucrat. I left them some materials and asked if I could come back in a few days with some more information. They didn't seem overjoyed with spending more time on the subject but told me that if I wanted to, "sure we can see you."

Getting dressed for the follow-up meeting, I took out the Purple Heart I was awarded for the time I was wounded in Germany and put the medal's lapel pin on my suit. The reception this time was quite different from the first time. I was no longer a mere government bureaucrat but an honored wounded veteran. The same people who had seemed so indifferent on the first visit now couldn't do enough to help me get the word out to their members.

It was a sartorial device I would use with all the other veteran organizations I visited with similar excellent results.

During the second year in Baltimore, Eileen was pregnant with our third child. After going to the doctor, I asked when she was scheduled for the caesarian and was as surprised as she had been when the doctor said there was no reason for another operation. If things went well during delivery, they would try for a natural birth. Years later, I found that a group of young doctors felt that normally healthy women who had undergone one caesarian birth could in all probability deliver their next child naturally. It was years later, based on the experience of these doctors, that it became an accepted practice.

But it was at the dinner table that I got an idea for my next venture. My young daughter, Ellen, was starting school. I began tossing an idea over in my mind. I wondered if I could interest the educational organizations in material for classroom use that would help teachers explain how the social security system works since many of the young people in schools would be entering the workplace either while they were still in school or after they were graduated.

So I proposed to Hink that I would approach the National Education Association and see if they would be interested in working with them in developing materials for classroom use. It took only one meeting at the NEA headquarters in downtown Washington to find out that the educators would be wholeheartedly behind any effort to develop teaching materials that could be offered to social science teachers.

To sweeten the deal, I offered to have the NEA experts review and approve any materials that social security would develop. The next step was to work with the graphic designers at headquarters to put together the package for NEA approval. What emerged was a package that included wall charts, publications and films that were advertised in a brochure that was distributed with the help of the enthusiastic professionals at the NEA.

In a very short time, schools all over the country were asking for and receiving the package of social security teaching materials. I was amazed at how fast word spread, and since the materials were free to the schools, how the demand boomed.

We were never too busy not to have fun with the bureaucracy. There were these little red stickers that were attached to memos that were important. They were red with white letters stating "SPECIAL", but over time just like the papers that were stamped "Confidential", their use proliferated. So, together with my friends in the graphics branch, we designed another label, this time purple. And the white letters screamed "FRANTIC." Soon they were used all over the organization until the brass sent out a notice that these stickers were not to be used.

Another ploy I undertook was to take the famous photograph of president Franklin Roosevelt signing the original social security act in 1934. The graphics people enlarged it and then forged FDR's signature inscribed to "Morton Lebow." It was framed and hung on the wall of my office without saying a word about it to anyone. I went about my work, and, eventually was visited by the flower and chivalry of the executive staff who suddenly had business with me. And never a word was said about the famous photograph.

I came down with a case of viral pneumonia which meant I became hors de combat for three weeks and largely confined to bed. Those were the days before the internet and tela-working, but I, with the help of my next door neighbor, Bill Gardner, found a way to keep up with my work. Each day, Bill would pick up everything from my office in box and leave it with me, and I would give to him for delivery to my office, the previous day's completed work. Those three weeks may have been one of the more productive periods of my career.

It was during those weeks that I began raising a well groomed beard which I thought I would display on my return to work. After getting the expected laughs and comments, I thought I would shave it off, but events intervened. Although almost everything went as expected, Roy Swift acted offended that one of his boys would come to work looking as a hippie. So I decided to keep it on.

As the office began preparations for our Christmas party, I was cast, with my beard, as the villain in the piece. Then, before the last act, when I would meet my just reward, I shaved off the beard and replaced it with a fake one we had modeled the day before. Then to the stage, where I was captured and the beard was torn from my face. There are still those who insist that I never had a real beard.

One day Charlotte Crenson and I were having lunch at a restaurant near the office. She excused herself for a moment, and when, she returned to the table, she was excited. She had run into a person who worked in the agency's accounting operation. He told her that he could identify everyone over 100 years of age who was getting social security. So Charlotte developed a whole public relations campaign around delivering the monthly checks with suitable publicity to all 112 recipients who were over 100 years of age. It would be years later when that number had blossomed to more than 10,000.

My assignments and work with national organizations kept me busy and interested, but after a while, my interest wandered. In working with so many varied groups, I became interested in how I could get some overall view of the impact the effort was making on the public. In musing over how I could get a handle on this, I eventually ended up going in two directions.

The office kept receiving newspaper clippings from the social security field offices. No one was in charge of reviewing them, but if any of them looked especially interesting or important, Hink or Roy would forward the clipping to the Commissioner or whoever they thought might be interested. I decided to see if I could collect all clippings as they came in and summarize what I found so that the office could then share the picture of newspaper coverage of the social security program with the entire executive staff on a regular basis.

The first thing was to send word out to all district offices that the public information office would welcome receiving newsworthy clippings. What I got was a deluge of clippings, most of which were of little note, but from this cascade, I was able to write up a report of the state of the nation's news about how the public viewed the social security program. I distributed the report about once a month and found that became a report that was expected and looked forward to.

As part of the shelf of books that came with the job was a ten pound book that gave summaries of all the public opinion polls conducted in the United States. From time to time, someone would ask me if I could find out what the public was thinking on this or that issue. One day, a newly hired information specialist, Milt Wisoff, came up to me and asked, "Someone said you had information about public opinion polls?"

"Yeah, I do. Why?"

"Well" Milt said, obviously bothered by something, "The guy who's giving the class for us new guys, said that the Social Security Act wasn't popular when it first came out and that it took some time before it was OK with the people."

I laughed and shook my head, "Nope, it was immensely popular from the start." And I pulled down the 10 pound book from the shelf and riffled through it until I found the polls from the mid-1930s when the Act was first debated and passed. I showed Milt the polls that usually showed about 90% approval ratings.

Milt asked if he could take the book to class the next day, and he happily walked off to class with it. When he returned later that afternoon, I asked him how things went.

"The bastard wouldn't call on me!"

That started another friendship, but it also started me thinking along a different line and wondered if the social security offices, if given the right materials and direction, could conduct their own surveys and find out where, if necessary, they could improve their operations. It was almost at the same time that a person in the regional office in Charlottesville came up with the same idea. So, after proposing the idea, to Hink, we went about lining up the necessary help to come up with material and logistics they would need. The people in the Statistics Branch would set up the sample that would be needed for a believable survey and would do the statistical analysis of the results. The Charlottesville Region lined up 26 offices to conduct the survey, and I struggled to come up with an acceptable survey questionnaire.

I knew very well that I was an amateur in this field, so I took a draft questionnaire over to Mrs. Trienah Meyers who worked in the Marketing Service at the Department of Agriculture. I found her, not only willing, but quite enthusiastic to help with the project. And between the two of us, a suitable questionnaire was designed. And off it went to the 26 field offices who conducted surveys in person, by mail and by telephone.

The results were encouraging. It showed that the offices could conduct reliable surveys of public knowledge and attitudes and showed clearly where more effort would have to be made in increasing public understanding. So, with the results all in, I presented the findings to the Executive Staff. I was more than disappointed when the top brass found fault with the excellent questions that showed lack of knowledge, but leapt to accept the answers to those questions that showed vast knowledge, even though those were the weakest.

But at least, we had demonstrated that such a survey could be used.

It was while the survey was being conducted in the field that the Social Security Administration was moving into their brand new building in the Baltimore suburbs, the decision was made to hold an open house for the community and staff families. They tapped me to plan the event.

51

Working with the graphics people, we developed a map that would be handed out to all the visitors for the open house which would let them do a self guided tour, with docents at each of the numbered stops to explain what was happening on working days. By all accounts, the day turned out to be a success as several thousand people toured the new building, and the map became a collector's item.

But I didn't have much time to bask in this latest venture. Social Security had been host to foreign visitors for many years usually the guests of specific officials of the agency, but lately, especially with the advent of the new headquarters, the flow of foreign visitors had increased. With this increase, came a need for someone to be added to the staff to handle the details of these visits. While the agency was recruiting for this position, they asked me if I could handle this until they hired someone permanently.

It was a temporary job that was going to change our lives in a way I had no way of forecasting. I realized very quickly that although the visitors received attention during working hours, they were in a foreign city on their own after business hours. It would make sense to ask for volunteers who would extend hospitality to these visitors after business hours. In short order, I had a list of more than one hundred people who would like to be the afterhours hosts. Eileen and I did our share of entertaining, usually having the visitors for dinner with a few of our friends. It was during these encounters that we spent some very pleasant evenings with representatives from Spain and the Philippines. Finally, someone was hired to take over the job, a Millard Langfeld who had come over from the State Department. As I explained the home visitation program, Millard asked, "You don't do this for Mrs. Anacic do you?"

Zagorka Anicic was a visitor from the census bureau in Yugoslavia.

"Millard, this woman is a guest of our country. We'll treat her just like we treat any other official guest."

"But she's a communist, and you'll be exposing our employees to a security risk. You don't want to do that."

I shook my head, "Millard, let the rest of the world go crazy, but not us."

And that was it until two days later when Roy Swift called me into his office for a consultation.

"Mort, Millard has raised a real problem about exposing our employees to a security issue if we have Mrs. Anicic mingle with them after hours."

"Roy, this woman is a guest of our country. To treat her differently from the rest would be a real insult."

The conversation went downhill from there and became really heated with no resolution in sight until I finally asked, "Are you ordering me not to extend this courtesy to Mrs. Anicic?"

"Yes, I am!"

"OK Roy, but don't tell me how to live my own life!"

And that was how they left it, but it wasn't going to rest there. I spoke to Charlotte Crenson and Milt Wisoff, and asked them if they would be willing to step in and spend time with Anicic after hours knowing that she was a communist from Yugoslavia. Of course, they both agreed, and between the three of us, we picked up the slack so that there was no noticeable break in the pattern of home hospitality. Because of this, Eileen and I became quite friendly with her for the rest of her life which included a few trips to Yugoslavia after she returned to her country.

But the affair left me with an uneasy feeling about my relationship with Roy Swift who, after all, was the boss of the office. And because of this uneasy feeling, when a friend, Ray Lannon, called and asked me if I wanted to be detailed to be the press officer for the White House Conference on Narcotics and Drug Abuse , I jumped at the chance. And our life took another major jump in direction.

Chapter Four

Our Best Compliment

1962-1966

It was there at The White House Conference that I met a guy named Bob Hutchings who would run the public affairs office for the Conference. Hutchings was on loan from the Public Health Service where he ran the public affairs office for the fairly new water pollution control efforts. He was a refugee from the private sector where he had worked for the J. Walter Thompson public relations organization.

I was assigned to handle the radio and television contacts for the conference, and I threw myself into the enterprise with all the energy I could muster. I arranged a number of interviews for the delegates to the conference and every day learned a little more from Hutchings about the ins and outs of dealing with the media.

It was during the conference that I, for the first and only time, deliberately lied to the press. At the time the conference was in session, down in Mississippi, a fellow named James Meredith, a black, was trying to enroll at the University of Mississippi. There were riots which threatened to widen unless the Federal Government intervened. Attorney General Robert Kennedy was due any moment to sit on a panel discussion. Several of the members of the press asked me which entrance the Attorney General was going to be using. I decided that Kennedy did not need to be waylayed during these tense moments, shrugged and pointed to the rear of the State Department auditorium saying, "I guess that's where he be coming in." It allowed the Attorney General to come in through the stage entrance and take his seat on the platform without interruption.

It was shortly after that when there was a moment I had a chance to observe an historic moment, the significance of which I was not to understand until many years later. As Kennedy seated himself, one of his aides plugged in a telephone near where I was standing. The telephone signal was a light rather than a bell. Midway through the panel talk, the light blinked. The aide listened and said, "I'll get him." He went over and whispered the message into Kennedy's ears. Kennedy nodded, and a short time later he left his seat and took the phone. I was standing nearby and heard only the Washington part of the conversation.

Kennedy listened and said, "No."

Listened some more, "I said no."

Once again, "Damn it. I said no!"

It were be years later that I was to understand the significance of what I had overheard. It was then, when reading about the events, I read that the federal marshals ,who were under attack by the mobs at the university, were asking permission to load their weapons.

And that was it. After the conference was over I returned to my job at social security, but Bob Hutchings and I kept in touch, because he wanted me to come over to the water pollution program as the press officer. At first, I resisted, because it would mean another move, this time from Baltimore to Washington, and Eileen, with the children in school, and showing a great deal of courage, had become a substitute teacher in junior high school in Baltimore County where she was in great demand.

But Hutchings was persistent and Eileen thought it would be a good move, so finally I agreed. When I told Hink that I was going to accept the offer, Hink wished me luck and told me he was sorry to lose me, but Roy Swift called me in and tried to induce me to stay with social security. I explained to Roy that I felt it was time for a change and thanked Roy for his support in the past, but I had given a commitment and that was that.

It was a move that opened a whole new vista for me.

The public information office in the fairly new water pollution control program was fairly small with Hutch leading the way. I was to handle the press, but first I had to acquaint myself to an entirely new bureaucracy. Unlike social security which had years to build up its structure, the water pollution program which was housed in the Public Health Service was still finding its way. One of the ways that Hutch took to get me started was to meet each of the office heads once a week to come up with a report that would be sent up through channels and ultimately to the White House with newsworthy events. And in a short time I became familiar with what the program was about.

But for the first three weeks, I wondered if I had made a mistake changing jobs, because Hutch had a habit of which Gertrude Stein would have approved. With his brilliant and fast mind, he would launch a sentence, and as soon as he thought the sense of it had gone through, he was on to the next one. It took me about three weeks to grasp this new rapid fire form of communication.

One of the branches in the Clean Water Program was the Enforcement Branch headed by Murray Stein. Murray, a former New Yorker, was not a PHS Commissioned Officer which I found, after working with him for a while, really bothered him. But he led the enforcement operations with determination. Under the Clean Water Act, the federal government could intervene with an enforcement conference if the government of one state complained that another state was polluting its waterway.

At each of the enforcement actions, I acted as the conduit between the Feds and the press. I quickly made sure that any prepared statements by any of the presenters would get into the hands of the press as quickly as possible. We also arranged interviews as we or the press wanted.

After a few of these actions, I felt I needed some help. It was fortunate that on the scene strolled a fellow who I knew briefly as a summer intern at Social Security. Adrian 'Duke' Sybor was a graduate from the University of Maryland School of Journalism and a refugee from the Associated Press in Annapolis, Maryland who was looking for another job. After chatting with him, I asked Hutch to chat with him saying I'd like to bring him on. it was one of my better decisions, because he turned out to be a talented self starter.

There were a number of enforcement actions on the nation's waterways we covered, but the one that taught me a lesson about checking the information I passed on to the press was about the pollution of the Mississippi River. There were reported massive fish kills in Louisiana. It was obvious to us that it was the result of agricultural runoff into the river, so I prepared the news release accordingly. It went over to the Department of

Agriculture for their assent but came back with the part about runoff deleted.

I was annoyed that we would cave in to Agriculture and let Hutch know my feelings. He calmed me down and pointed out that the release was only a piece of paper, but it was hunting license to peddle the story. And it was just as well, because the pollution turned out not to be coming from runoff but from a company in Memphis, Velsicol, which was dumping used chemicals on the flood plain outside their plant.

It was then that I learned to check the accuracy of information that was being passed on to the press. Murray Stein told me that Velsicol wasn't allowing our investigators into their plant. Accepting this, I passed it on to the *NY Times* reporter who checked with the company and found that our investigators had just finished their inspections. That reporter would never trust me again, and I didn't blame him.

The enforcement conference took place in New Orleans, and Stu Lowery, a reporter for the *New York Herald Tribune* told me how to stay at the luxurious Royal Orleans Hotel on a federal worker's per diem. And the city lived up to its afterhours reputation. The food at marvelous restaurants and the music at Preservation Hall were all that I could expect.

It was months later when we were planning for an enforcement action on the Snake River that we received our best compliment. Word was passed to us through the congressional delegation from Idaho that the press officers were not to be allowed to attend. So we arranged for Peter Kuh, Stein's deputy, to be in touch with us by phone during the course of the conference, and guided him as he dealt with the press out there.

One day, I received a call from our Great Lakes Project manager who asked me to come to Chicago to review some of their findings. It was there that a new word "eutrophication" entered my vocabulary. The staff of the project briefed me on what they found in their study of Lake Erie. They found that one quarter of the bottom of the lake had eutrophied.

At that point, I held up my hand," What does that mean?"

"It means that 25 percent of the bottom of the lake has no oxygen."

"So?"

"It means that the algae will grow there and eventually take over the lake. If this continues to happen, Lake Erie can very well become a bog."

Then I began to get a glimmer of what eutrophication would mean to the water supply of that huge industrial area around the great lakes. After a much longer discussion where they briefed me on the ins and outs of their study, I returned to Washington to brief Hutch. We gathered together with the PHS engineers in our program and decided that the first step was to draft a news release reporting the findings and mapping out a program to try to reduce the pollution of industrial wastes that were pouring into Lake Erie.

The draft news release was sent up to the Department office for final clearance. It was there that we ran into a brick wall. Jim Quigley, a former congressman from Pennsylvania, the Assistant Secretary for Health at the time, rejected the news release because, Secretary Anthony Celebreese, had been the former mayor of Cleveland, and "It wouldn't look good for him and his record."

It was then that Hutch showed me how to become a disloyal government employee when acting for the public good.

First, he got in touch with some officials of the League of Women Voters with whom we had a working relationship. He found that the League chapter in Ohio was going to have a meeting in Cleveland in a few weeks. He suggested that they invite the director of our Great Lakes Project to give a presentation there. Once they agreed and extended the invitation, I called the *NY Times* correspondent who was covering the pollution beat. Gladwin Hill was a veteran reporter who had served in Europe reporting during World War II and had been working with us on several stories. I told him about the meeting that was scheduled for Cleveland and suggested very strongly that he attend.

"You're going to get a good story out of that meeting, Glad."

And he attended along with a reporter from the *Cleveland Plain Dealer*. We never did issue a news release, but we didn't have to, because the publicity that the stories filed by Gladwin Hill and the reporter from the *Plan Dealer* went viral long before the days of the internet.

What followed, of course, was an enforcement conference which resulted in an entire course of actions which, amazingly, did halt the progress of that indecipherable term --eutrophication.

Then, one day, our world was turned upside down. As I was doing some paperwork at my desk, Sam Levinson, one of our writers, came in with a stricken look on his face. as I looked up, he said with shock in his voice, "the president's been shot!" I must have sat there agape, because he nodded, "Yes, he was in Dallas." I got up from my desk leaving the now useless paperwork and quickly ran over to the North Building of HEW where the information office had a ticker tape. It was with these that we could see the whole story unfold. Any thought of work for that and the next few days disappeared.

It was some time after the Lake Erie story and the Kennedy assassination that we were involved with an enforcement conference on the Hudson

River. It was being held at a time of the great newspaper strike in New York. The only paper that wasn't on strike was the *Herald Tribune*. Duke and I worked overtime to interest the TV and radio stations in the event along with the newspapers from New Jersey and Long Island. I even tried to get the Washington papers--the *Post* and the *Star*--interested in attending. Although the *Post* wasn't interested, Orr Kelly of the *Star* agreed that we could feed him information by phone, and that's what we did.

Duke went ahead to handle the preliminary work before the Conference started. It was there that he accompanied Senator Robert Kennedy on an inspection trip out on the river. He witnessed Kennedy receiving a call asking him to get back to his New York office. As a launch came alongside their vessel to take Kennedy back to shore, Duke heard him say, as he was stepping from one boat to the launch, "If I fall in, I won't drown, I'll probably dissolve."

The conference was held in the Starlight Room of the Waldorf Astoria. The large Waldorf Room was connected to our equally large press room by a much narrower corridor with a bank of elevators. It was there that Senator Kennedy was going to give me a lesson on how to hold a news conference.

As Kennedy was getting ready for his presentation at the head of the room, I approached him and said, "Senator, the press would like to be able to talk to you." We agreed that I would give him a signal at a break in the proceedings, and he would come out for the hastily arranged press conference.

At a break, I signaled him, and he rose up and started walking toward the doors leading out of the conference room. And it seemed as if an act of the Pied Piper was being held with almost half the audience rose and following him. It was in the connecting corridor which, by this time, was jammed with people that he taught me my lesson.

He said, "Let's do it here."

I started to object that the press room was set up when I realized he had much better instincts than I did. The pictures that would come out on TV and in the few papers that were covering it, would show the Senator with people pressing around him as he took and answered questions rather than the antiseptic setting of a podium in the press room with no background to speak of.

Aside from the events that were forced on me to cover such as the enforcement conferences and the reports from our projects, there were other ways to make the program interesting.

One day, I was chatting with Orr Kelly, the reporter from the *Evening Star*, and mentioned that we received a lot of correspondence from children who often gave us their suggestions of how to solve the problem of water pollution. He seemed interested, so I collected a group of these letters including some with drawings. What followed was a charming story with some of the drawings prominently displayed across the bottom of the front page.

The next day, Stu Auerback from the *Post* came in to do the story. I laughed, "Stu the story's been done."

"I know," he replied, "but my editors don't."

Our engineers were preparing to set up a series of monitors to measure pollution on the Potomac River. One of these monitors was to be installed beneath the Memorial Bridge. We then prepared to hold a news event beneath the bridge. The media hired boats to cover the event with TV cameras and reporters on board. Not knowing what we'd see, I followed the engineers down from the entrance at the middle of the bridge and saw the huge concrete counterweights that were used to raise and lower the bridge when it served as the drawbridge to allow ships to go up river to the then Port of Georgetown.

Some time later, I came across a report about a sanitary engineer at a small community just east of San Diego who was buying the waste water from San Diego, super treating it, and using it to supply the water for his town. To demonstrate how safe this retreated water was, he even used it for the town's swimming pool. Then, after the water had been used, he sold it to nearby golf courses for irrigation and received more funds than he had spent to buy the water from San Diego in the first place. I mentioned it to Glad, who lived and worked in Los Angeles, so we arranged a trip with Glad driving to see if this fairy tale was real. It was and made it into the *New York* Times a few days later.

Another time, when I was in Los Angeles, there had been an outbreak of Salmonella in Riverside. What was unusual was that the infection had been identified as coming from Riverside's drinking water. And that water came from deep wells where the general wisdom said that salmonella could not exist, but the expert from the Centers for Disease Control (CDC) who was assigned to California had eliminated all other sources of contamination.

I checked with Glad and suggested that there might be as story here, so the both of us took a drive down to Riverside where we spoke to the city's sanitary engineer. He was completely at a loss since he knew that the cold water from his deep wells should not have been the cause of the outbreak, but faced with the very convincing evidence from the man from CDC, he had to reluctantly admit that it could be possible. It was several days later that at a meeting of almost all of California's sanitary engineers, the CDC representative presented his findings to a still skeptical audience. And it was several days after that an article with Gladwin Hills by-line appeared in the *NY Times*.

It was still while I was in Los Angeles that I received a phone call from Hutch who informed me that he was being offered the job of Public Information Officer for the new office that was being organized to publicize the dangers of cigarette smoking. It was going to be a challenging job fighting the headwinds of the tobacco companies lobby, but he wanted to let me know, and, I thought odd, he wanted to know if I would mind being left behind to run the water pollution office. He had spoken to Stewart Hunter, the Public Information officer for the PHS and the Surgeon General, and Stu had given me his blessing to step into Hutch's shoes.

Stew Hunter was another former employee at the J. Walter Thompson public relations firm and a former naval officer who had seen service in the Pacific notably on an aircraft carrier during the Battle of Midway that so changed the course of the war in the Pacific. During the few years I had been working with Hutch, I had worked with Stew, and we had formed a close and warm working relationship, so the blessing really did not come out of the blue.

During the time I worked with Hutch he introduced me to the world of public service TV announcements. Every year, he ,with the help of John Daly the TV personality, would, working with a PR firm, develop a public service announcement promoting the clean water program. It was shortly after Hutch had left that our PR firm came to me with an idea for such an announcement.

Using the song "Pollution" that had been written by Tom Lehrer, they proposed to have Lehrer perform the song on the PSA. I wrote to Lehrer asking him if he would perform it for us. Not hearing from him for some time, I phoned him. He told me that under no conditions would he perform it. He had seen himself on TV once and didn't like what he saw. We could use the song as a public service and pay nothing, but not him. It would be OK if we got some actor to do the job.

With that, I began to go down the list of possible performers we could get. One name that stood out was that of Zero Mostel. His agent was his brother who was a CPA in New York, so we set up an appointment and showed up at his office explaining what we would like to do. Zero's brother, who looked much like Zero, then wrote a note on a yellow pad, "Zero, your government wants you to do something for them."

Only a few days later, word came back. He would be glad to do the spot after he finished filming "A Funny Thing Happened on the Way to the Forum" in England. The excitement that followed should have been anticipated, Tom Lehrer said he would rewrite the lyrics if Mostel wanted him to. Our PR outfit would assign their top producer to the job. We all waited with great anticipation. But, sadly, it was not to be.

Jim Quigley, who had squashed the Lake Erie news release, was installed as the Director of the water pollution control program, He called a staff meeting to discuss how he saw the program. During the meeting, he addressed me and said that even though I was there when Hutchings was running the public information program, he knew I wasn't the one making the final decisions. I couldn't let that pass and replied that although I wasn't in charge I agreed with all the major decisions made and thought they strengthened the program. I sort of guessed that I was signing my death warrant as far as the program under Quigley was concerned.

A short time later, we were ready to start up the program to monitor pollution levels on the Potomac River. I prepared brief remarks for Quigley to use at the news conference. He glanced at the page and a half and stuffed them in his pocket. I assumed he was going to wing it on his own and was amazed as he gave his short talk word for word as I had written in the draft--a truly remarkable feat.

It wasn't long after that that we were called to a large meeting in the Department's auditorium. The entire professional staff of the organization was there to hear Secretary John Gardiner tell us that he had agreed to move the water pollution control program to the Department of Interior. It would mean leaving the Public Health Service.

Although I had enjoyed working with the PHS people, particularly Stew Hunter, I was prepared to make the change until Quigley announced that Charlie Rogers, the Press Officer for HEW would take that position within the new department. Realizing that I would be a thorn in his side, I checked with Hunter to see if there was a job for me in the PHS and found that indeed there was. So I visited the public information man at Interior to tell him I would not be transferring with the program.

He tried to dissuade me saying they would carve out a special position for me, but I had made my mind up. He then said, "Glad Hill wrote me a letter about you." He seemed surprised that I hadn't known about it, but he handed me a copy and told me I could keep it. When I read the letter, I was moved and amused to read a letter that urged him to keep me on board at any costs. I, of course, had a chance to thank him later on.

Chapter Five

The HEW Shuffle

1966-1970

The job Stew Hunter had in mind for me was a fascinating one. Lyndon Johnson after he became president pushed through two major laws. They were the Civil Rights Act of 1964 and the equally important Medicare Act to extend health care insurance to all seniors who had worked long enough to qualify. Any health facility that wanted to participate in the Medicare program had to comply with Title VI of the Civil Rights Act which barred discrimination on the basis of race, color or national origin.

Of the almost 7,500 hospitals in the country the vast majority complied with these provisions quite easily. In fact, more than 7,000 had already qualified. It was with the remaining four or five hundred that we were going to have the most trouble.

Leading the effort for the PHS was the Deputy Surgeon General, a rather genial commissioned officer who was a stickler for details. My introduction to Leo Gehrig was to clear a news release with him. A few people in the office smiled knowingly as I departed for my first encounter with this man. And it was quite an encounter, because he went over the release almost word for word and had comments along the way. Although I was shaken at the idea of having to work with him, I came to value his firmness and integrity as he led the program to bring fairness to the way the health facilities in our country treated our citizens.

The program to integrate the nation's hospitals was an immense task. We had to visit almost 3,000 hospitals to make sure they were in compliance. Very shortly, our investigators ran into what we called the "HEW SHUFFLE" where white and negro patients were moved into new beds and new wards to make it look as if the hospital was in compliance but were moved back into segregated situations once the Fed left.

This led, on more than one occasion, to an almost comical situation. One team member, a very distinguished looking gentleman stopped at a local coffee shop before he visited the local hospital. While he was sitting sipping his coffee, a man came in and sat down near him. The fellow working the counter came up to him and said, "How are things going George?" George replied, "Oh, not so good. Some of those damn civil rights guys are coming up to look at the hospital today. But I got things fixed up so that we'll pass the inspection. I put some negroes in over to the white ward and some of the white guys in the negro ward, I even told some of our colored workers to come down and eat in the cafeteria today."

Our guy cleared his throat a few times. George and the counterman looked over toward him. About half an hour later when our guy walked into the hospital administrator's office, he was greeted with the most double take he had ever seen.

While our investigators were busy in the field, I was busy writing news releases tallying up our progress in signing up hospitals. There was a chart we kept in the office to help reporters keep track for their stories. It listed state by state: total hospitals, number approved and number still unapproved. Also there were news releases telling of individual hospitals that were not in compliance.

One of these was the large Mobile Infirmary in Mobile Alabama. Initially, they informed us that they weren't interested in participating in Medicare, but as more and more of their patients began to complain about having to shell out their own money for their care, the administrator asked us to come down to see if we could work something out. It was there that I saw Dr. Leo Gehrig at his best.

Sitting around the table, in addition to our delegation which included Dr. Gehrig in his full commissioned officer's uniform, were all the members of the hospital board. It was obvious that they weren't the happiest bunch of people I had ever seen. After some time of listening to their various reasons why it wouldn't be advisable integrate the hospital all at once, Dr. Gehrig pointed out that the physicians were referring their white patients to the Infirmary while sending their black patients to the lone black hospital. One board member who seemed to speak for all of them, said, "You mean to tell us that we have to tell our doctors how to practice medicine?"

"Not at all" Gehrig answered, "but I know that you can discipline a doctor if he doesn't keep up two patients' medical chart. If you can do that, you can tell him not to break the law by assigning his patients in a discriminating manner!"

That was the turning point in the discussion. Working with the hospital administrator, the hospital changed its practices and eventually came into full compliance.

While we were in Mobile, Dr. Gehrig and I visited the lone Doctors Hospital to explain what was needed to begin receiving Medicare funds. We were greeted politely and told just as politely that they were not interested in participating. It was less than a month later that we received word that they had changed their minds.

After our visits and before we left Mobile our group met in a bar for some drinks and to talk over our experiences. One of our members Dr. Mike Holloman from the New York City Health Department was accompanied by his white girlfriend. Since Dr. Holloman was black, I held my breath at the waitress came to take our orders and was amazed and relieved when she greeted us cheerfully and served us with courtesy. Times were changing.

Back in DC, we kept tallying the progress. There were still a few holdouts. There was one especially troubling one in Philadelphia, Mississippi. Our investigators could not find them out of compliance, although we knew we were being hoodwinked. A young black activist visited our office, and, as I discussed our predicament with him, he admitted that his group had the evidence we needed to hold the hospital out of compliance; but he was not willing to give that evidence to us. I explained that we were going to have to approve the hospital unless we got evidence that they were flouting the law. He nodded his head and shrugged his shoulders and told me that they were holding that evidence to use in a lawsuit they would go ahead with.

Eventually, the work of getting the health facilities into compliance was winding down and Stew Hunter moved me into his office in the Office of the Surgeon General. It was there one day that I saw something that was hard to believe.

Charles M. Schulz, the creator of the Peanuts comic strip had offered to donate his strip about Amblyopia Ex Anopsia, lazy eye, to the PHS for our use in calling attention to that condition and how to remedy it. The National Center for Chronic Disease Control was about to decline the offer. Finding that hard to believe, I asked Stew if those people were out of their heads. He spoke to the head of the Center and got them to change their minds and accept the offer. The lovely and funny 13 page pamphlet that emerged, "Security is an Eye Patch" was an instant success with the acknowledgement on the inside front cover to Schultz and the United Features Syndicate for "Their courtesy and public spiritedness."

After several months, there was an upheaval in that office. In a monumental miscalculation, Carl Spitzer, the Assistant Secretary for Public Affairs, inserted another person in Stew's position and moved Stew downtown to set up the Department's Information Center to handle the initial procedures for administering the newly enacted Freedom of Information law.

After a short time, Stew asked for me to be assigned to that office. It was there that we set up the Information Center and set up the procedures for the Freedom of Information Act (FOIA). As we went about establishing the exhibits that would be the centerpiece of the Center, I began collecting copies of the original congressional legislations that were the basis for the Department of Health, Education and Welfare. I had requested from the National Archives a copy of the Act in 1920 that authorized the Food and Drug Administration. When it arrived, it was an Indian Treaty Act on the same date as the FDA Act. I called my contact at the Archives who was very apologetic and rushed over by special messenger the proper act.

Then, looking at the signatures on the two acts, I saw what could be a great PhD Thesis. Both acts had Woodrow Wilson's name on them, but they were two different signatures. This was after Wilson's strokes. So which one was his signature and which one was his wife's. I never found out, but was left wondering if some PhD candidate could scour the archives for all legislation signed after his stroke and with a handwriting expert determine which ones really had the strength of law.

Late one morning, a heavyset middle aged man came to the information center. After chatting with this foreign accented man, I found that he was from Russia and a cancer researcher who was heading for a meeting at the Cancer Institute that afternoon. Finding that he was at loose ends for lunch, I asked him if he wanted to join me, and he immediately and enthusiastically accepted my offer. We walked up the hill to the lunchroom in the Longworth Office Building at the Capital. After lunch, I took him to the shuttle bus that would take him out to the NIH campus but not before he thrust a bottle of Vodka at me as a token of his appreciation.

I thought nothing of this pleasant meeting until two days later when two FBI agents appeared who wanted to talk with me. It was a good guy-bad guy routine. After I told them of the gentleman's visit, I mentioned, "Then we went to lunch." It was as if I had set off a bomb. Both agents almost rose from their chairs as one asked, "What did you talk about?"

"Well, we talked about the traffic in Washington and Moscow."

Then they wanted to know why I was certain he was who he said he was, and I responded that he seemed to be knowledgeable about cancer and the research that was going on. And that was that. I told Stew after they left that if the Soviets wanted to really tie up the FBI, they should send over a lot of tourists who would visit government offices.

There was one other notable effort we undertook before I left the information center. Sometime after the Watts riots in Los Angeles, the author Budd Shulberg organized the Watts Writers Workshop. Shulberg, living in upscale Bel Air, watched the riots unfold on TV and felt he wanted to do something, he didn't know what to do at first, to help these people. He decided to try to do what he knew best, so he went to Watts and searched around until he found a bar that would let him set up a table with a sign inviting writers to come and show him their work. He sat there for several weeks with no response.

Then, one day, a man approached the table and plunked down a manuscript of a short story before he fled. Shulberg reviewed the manuscript editing it very lightly and found that the man had a room over the bar which they gave him in return for his work cleaning up the place. Shulberg went up to the man's room the following week to discuss the short story and was amazed to see shelves made of crates filled with paperback books of all kinds.

And that was the beginning of the Watts Writers Workshop.

In addition to the publicity he generated for his effort, Shulberg also was able to market a collection of writings by residents of Watts which was published under the title of *From the Ashes*. I had read the book and couldn't help but being impressed by the quality of the writing by this group of hereto unknown authors, and wondered if we could find some way to hire them to write some government pamphlets. Hopefully, the finished products would be in the vernacular rather than in governmentaleese.

I wrote to Budd Shulberg with the proposition to see if he would be interested, It was a few days later that I received a phone call from the excited author saying he would be delighted to engage in the project with me. I told him that I would have to arrange the financing for the project and once I did, I would be in touch. There were four programs that were willing to take part in the effort giving me $1,000 for each pamphlet. I approached Ray Lannon who was now working in the Department's administration office and asked him how I could handle the finances. Ray, being a bureaucrat who always wanted to see how you could do things, came up with an easy way for me to go forward giving me a book of vouchers that I could use to contract for the work warning me that I was now responsible for those vouchers.

The next step was to set up a meeting with the Workshop at Shulberg's home in Bel Air. After reading *From the Ashes*, I had some ideas of which writers I would like for each of the four pamphlets. As the group gathered in Bel Air, it was very interesting to watch as Shulberg melted into the background and became just another observer rather than the person who would lead the meeting. It was obvious that he deliberately choose to cede all leadership to the writers from Watts.

I explained that I had the authorization to contract with them for writing the four pamphlets and explained that after reading their book, I would like to make the assignments. The first one was the pamphlet on alcoholism and I chose one of the writers. When I announced my choice, everyone in the room laughed. At first, I must have looked puzzled before it dawned on me that the person I chose did indeed have a drinking problem.

As soon as I could, I told him that he didn't have to do it, if he didn't wish, but laughing he said he would like to take it on, so we signed the first contract. The other three went off with no hitch. I would have liked to have the pamphlets designed by artists in Watts, but the Graphics office in HEW would not give permission for that.

Unfortunately, the finished products, although well written and easily readable came out as straightforward government pamphlets. It was a good idea that, at least, gave four writers from Watts some visibility and some cash and did produce some readable material.

It was some time after that very interesting and desirable experience that Ed McVeigh who had replaced Stew Hunter as Director of Public Affairs for PHS said he wanted me back in his office since I really had just been on loan to the Department. I wasn't looking forward to the move when fate and another of my friends stepped in.

Chapter Six

The Biggest Bar Mitzvah

1970

The 1970 White House Conference on Children and Youth was scheduled to take place in December with the Department of Health Education and Welfare selected to organize and run the affair. These conferences had a long and fairly influential history dating from the first one during Teddy Roosevelt's administration that led to many of our child labor laws.

A friend of mine, Charles Miller, from Social Security days, was assistant to the Assistant Secretary for Administration. They were looking for someone who would be the Executive Officer for the Conference and asked me to take the job. My first response was, "What do I know about being an Executive Officer?" but he assured me that they would back me up. So feeling this would be a reprieve from having to go back to the information office in PHS, I agreed.

It was a new learning experience as I dealt with personnel and budget matters, but with Charlie's help, I began to get the scheme of things. It was going along fairly well when the White House decided to send over Steve Hess to be the Director of the Conference.

We had a fellow on the staff as a fund raiser whose name was Tom Nunan. He was a former Roman Catholic priest from Mobile, Alabama where he had been active in the civil rights activities. He, very naively, had given the name of the local Republican congressman as a reference. And that congressman told the White House that under no conditions were they to have anything to do with him. Although Tom was due to give his report on his fund raising plan to the staff the following day, Steve Hess, following orders from the White House, told me to get rid of him.

I protested and said, "At least let him give his report and see what he says."

Steve agreed, but terminated his employment with the Conference immediately after Tom had his say. I asked Tom why he had given the congressman as a reference, and, showing a naivety that was amazing for a former priest, he said, "Well even though we had our differences, we were always civil with each other, and he agreed to give me a reference."

"Good God" I replied and laughed, "He didn't say what kind of reference he was going to give you."

It was shortly after that when Steve asked me to come to his office for a meeting. He told me that he wanted me to step aside for an executive director he wanted to bring on. I told him not to worry since I had a job to go back to, but he wanted me to stay on and offered me the public information job which I declined since someone was already in that job, and I wasn't about to "step over anyone's body." He then made me another offer. Would I take over the job as Director of Special Events with the challenge of making the Conference interesting. Agreeing to take the job with the understanding that it was more than just organizing special events, I was about to step into an entirely new world.

The first thing I had to do was to set up my own staff. Making the decision very early to operate with a small staff so that people wouldn't get in each others' way, I was lucky to have a young woman, Sharon, assigned as my secretary. Sharon was a short very slim and very dedicated person. Her shorthand and typing skills were supplemented by a very quiet intelligence. And her concern for other people showed up at a later crucial time.

Another addition to the staff was a fellow named Jim Den Boer who had come over from the PHS. I had run into him there and knew he was a quiet but bright person aside from the fact that he was a recognized poet. He agreed to come on as my backup. The fourth and final member of our team was Victor Margolin who I tabbed to develop the motion picture aspect of the conference. As time went on, Victor would come to me for direction, and I would always tell him to use his own discretion in making decisions. Eventually, he caught on and developed a very expansive series of showings.

As the planning for the conference was moving ahead, events on the other side of the world were going to have a significant effect on the way we organized the meeting. The United States forces in Vietnam were fighting what would eventually be a losing cause. They were winning individual battles, but the enemy was dominating the landscape outside the population centers. The anti-war movement in our country was gaining momentum.

I guess it was because of this that the Conference which traditionally had been the White House Conference and Children and Youth was broken up into two with the Conference on Children dealing with those 13 and younger scheduled in Washington for December of 1970 and the Conference on Youth scheduled for Estes Park, Colorado for February the following year. That was one way for the Nixon Administration to keep the major protestors as far from the Capital and the news as possible.

As we got underway, the new public information director, Mary Nell York, enlisted Ivan Chermioff, a well known graphic designer, to design a logo for the conference. He came up with two delightful red flowers with green leaves and presented it to us for consideration. I sat there at the staff meeting where the logo was under consideration with growing unease as the staff members became design experts and began tearing this delightful design to pieces. Finally, I had enough.

"Look, this is a very lovely design, And it exists just for the conference and not beyond. The only time a logo has any real influence is if it is used over time and is wedded to an ongoing program like Smoky the Bear that identifies the Forest Service." And then copying a tactic that I had seen Bob Hutchings use, I asked, "Now you all know what Department Smoky the Bear is from?" When everyone nodded and said, "The Department of Interior," I added, "It's really the Department of Agriculture, so there is no reason not to adopt this lovely logo." And that was that. The logo was a complete success for the duration of the conference and then disappeared into the archives.

One of the first things we did was to sign up a firm to handle the exhibits for the conference. The outfit we selected had been in the business for some time and had handled exhibit programs for other large government conferences. They would publicize the meeting and take care of all details of contracting with exhibitors. We would lay out no funds, but would reap the financial benefit after the company took their commission. The publicity brochure they sent out prominently displayed our delightful logo, and everyone commented on how bright and cheerful it looked.

We also began to find ways to attract conference goers to the exhibit floor, so we reached out to groups that would have an interest in making small presentations on the exhibit floor. These eventually included presentations from Sesame Street, young artists a comic strip artist and a sculptor among others. While searching for groups that would be willing to be presenters, I was referred to a fellow, Al Duca, who lived at Ammisquan on the North Cape near Boston.

Al was an accomplished sculptor who also had a great social conscience. He had arranged with the juvenile court to allow young people who were on parole for minor offensives to serve their time as assistants with him while working on big projects. Over time, as I negotiated with him to take part in the conference, I would visit him in his workshop where he would turn me over to one of his delinquents to explain what they were doing. And it became obvious that these young people who now had artistic responsibilities had become proud of what they were accomplishing.

But as we floundered around a bit, we decided that we were going to have two overriding responsibilities. The first was to come up with a comprehensive plan for how the conference would unfold; and the second would be to organize the special events that would adorn the conference.

As we studied how other conferences had been run, we began to come up with a general idea of how we were going to make this conference different from others, and, over time, the plan for the conference began to take shape. The plan we ultimately presented to Steve Hess and the staff was entitled, "Blueprint for Excitement." The major point was that no one would give a prepared, written speech. If anyone had a speech to give, they would give it to us and we would duplicate it for distribution. So no more dull, boring speeches to put the audience to sleep. We also gave a list of some 15 ways each section could present their ideas.

In keeping with the idea of making the presentations less formal, there would be no formal dinners or luncheons, but the members would be encouraged to continue their discussions among themselves in settings they chose. The various sections in which the conference was divided were encouraged to move out of the hotel premises and meet at locations that had some relevance to the problems they were addressing. And we also encouraged the sections to come up with a program that could be left to continue after the conference was over.

The idea of a conference without prepared speeches shocked some of the staff, because "that's the way it was always done." But this unusual conference design was eventually adopted and turned out to be exciting and engrossing. The conference expanded to locations in all parts of Washington--schools, hospitals, welfare organizations and a host of other venues. Some even stayed in the hotel.

With the general organization of the conference decided on, we became focused on the several special events that would dress up the place. Victor was putting together a film program that eventually would have showings of films by young people, for young people and films about them.

With Jim putting together the official program for the conference which featured art by young people for each of the sections, I turned my attention to seeing if we could stage a musical which would be entitled "the Sounds of Children." For this, I approached the Music Educators National Conference which was part of the NEA. They were more than willing to join with the White House Conference, and an organization meeting was arranged at their headquarters.

It was there that I met Kathryn Dunham, a dancer whom I had admired in my younger days. She had introduced African rhythms into modern dance and was now running a dance program in the slums of East St. Louis. Louis Werson, from the Philadelphia public schools would become one of the producers of the show. It was at this meeting where we identified the groups of young people who would be the stars of the show, and where I would make one of my mistakes.

One of the members of the organizing committee was Peggy Cafritz who would go on to be the organizer of her brainchild, the Duke Ellington School for the Performing Arts. After we had settled on the groups that would performing, she took me aside and pointed out that there were no groups from the District of Columbia. It was many years later when I was able to acknowledge to her that I had made a mistake.

Realizing that we were amateurs at producing a musical show, I turned to a friend who had been at City College with me. Ed Greenberg was the producer of the St. Louis Municipal Light Opera Company and the Los Angeles Light Opera Company with a great many shows under his belt. He readily agreed to come on, and having him was one of the best things we could do. He decided that we would should start the show very quietly and build up to a raucous finale. He was looking for someone who would play the dulcimer, and the music educators came through with a delightful young woman, Ruth McLain of Hyndman Kentucky.

While we were organizing the show, I was called to a meeting at the Sheraton Hotel with President Nixon's advance man and someone from the Secret Service to discuss the President's participation which up until now had been a closely held secret. As the advance man talked about where to place the Marine Band, I expressed disbelief.

"This is a conference for young people! And we have a band from Atlanta that could do the job."

"But can they play Hail To the Chief and Ruffles and Flourishes?"

When I answered that they could, the Secret Service man almost came out of his chair demanding "why?"

I answered with some amusement that this WAS a White House Conference. It was then that the advance man inserted himself. "Can we bring them up here and audition them?"

I tried not to laugh and said, "There are 97 of them, but I have a tape you can listen to." I called Sharon and asked her to grab a taxi and bring the tape and a recorder. It was on the opening night of the conference when the Atlanta Youth Band had played both required numbers that Nixon, always the politician, said, "I've heard those played hundreds of times but never have I heard them played so well." And I guess he would have gotten a couple of hundred votes from the parents and relatives who heard those remarks, and I'm pretty sure the advance man took the credit for having the Atlanta Youth Band do the honors.

The morning after the opening session and the president's speech on welfare reform, I was sitting with Steve Hess going over the day's program when he received a call from the White House. Sitting across the room from him, I could hear someone shouting at Steve over the phone. I gathered that the person was demanding to know why the report of the speech was on page three of the *NY_Times* and not on page one. Steve, quite subdued, said, "I can't tell them where to put it." Then even though I was across the room, I heard a primordial shout "Why not?" It was several years later on a shuttle flight from New York to Washington that I asked him whether it was Haldeman or Ehrlichman. He looked at me and replied, "That was the President."

As the music program took shape, Ed drew up plans for the stage. He envisioned a central stage and two smaller ones on each side in front of the main stage. As Ed was planning the show, I was searching for someone who could be a master of ceremonies. The music educators suggested that I see if a young conductor in Boston, Michael Tillson Thomas, would be interested. I flew up to Boston and met with him explaining about the show and emphasizing that I wanted someone to introduce the young performers but not to overshadow them. He listened politely and declined saying that he did not wish to be connected with anything involving Richard Nixon.

It was then that Kathryn Dunham came to my rescue. She suggested that we ask Marge Champion, half of the dancing team of Marge and Gower Champion. I called her and explained what we wanted again emphasizing that I did not want someone who would overshadow the kids. And, luckily, she agreed, because she turned out to be a life saver during rehearsals.

Ed planned the show with Ruth McLain leading off with her quiet dulcimer singing folk songs of rural Kentucky gradually building with excitement and sound until the show ended with a group of loud rock sounds from four young people the New Borns from East St. Louis on the small stage on the left. He also would station a group of bell ringers from Philadelphia on the steps at the entrance to the hall who would ring the audience in.

We had reached out to the television networks to see if any of them would be interested in covering the event, and NBC with their Saturday morning children's show eagerly came on board. In making the arrangements with them, we agreed that they would have complete freedom to film during the rehearsal but would be confined to a platform toward the rear of the hall during the show.

In the midst of the lead up to the preparation for the show, Sharon, quite upset, came to me. The reservations for the members of the Atlanta band had gone astray, and they had no place to stay for one night. She had located another hotel that could take them for one night and wanted to know if it was OK to make the reservation. She did and the next night, the Sheraton Hotel, to make up for the glitch, put the band in several excellent suites.

As we began the rehearsal, Marge Champion asked if she could chat with each act and come up with her comments as mistress of ceremonies. I was more than delighted to give her free reign rather than have Ed and I try to give her a script that night. And she did her job as the professional that she was.

During the rehearsal there were two moments that required some intervention. The first occurred when a group of young men from East St. Louis were rehearsing their act demonstrating judo routines and were going on much too long. I mentioned this to Kathryn and, much to my surprise, she asked me if I would speak to the coach, a man. Then I realized that although Kathryn ran the dance group, in East St. Louis, she was living in a man's world. So I approached the coach and told him that, although their routine was very interesting, after about two minutes the audience attention would begin going elsewhere. He took my manly advice to heart and cut down the routine to acceptable length.

The other, and most important moment, came when Louis Werson from the Music Educators wanted the show to end with all 250 some odd performers on the stage singing "God Bless America." As Ed was trying to set this, Kathryn, quite upset, pulled me aside and said, "Mort, my kids won't sing it!" I told her that I would check with Ed. I pulled him aside and whispered, "Ed, Kathryn's kids won't sing it."

He waved me aside and said, "Tell her not to worry."

When I relayed the message, she was about to say something, but I assured her that Ed would take care of it. Actually, he found that it was not working the way Werson wanted, so he told the New Borns that after they took their bows, they should stay in place. When the lights came on, they were to start playing again anything they wanted. He then told the other acts when they heard the New Borns starting to play again, anyone who wanted to could come onto the stage and start dancing. On the night of the performance, when the children rushed onto the stage to dance, there was another rush with people from the audience coming onto the stage to join the dance with the young people for a lovely and exciting ending to the show.

I had just one other job to do before wrapping up my tenure with the conference. On two days after the performance of "The Sounds of Children," the conference would have the last of the section meetings. I had approached the US Information Agency about using their TV studios to record Steve Hess and the other leaders so that all sections that were meeting separately could watch their final report. It was there that I had run into a group of bureaucrats who delighted in saying "No." They explained that they, by law, were not allowed to broadcast in the United States, Using the influence of the White House name, I finally got them to agree to use their studios and personel to record the final report to the sections. I also was able to contract with a studio in Washington to take the tape after we finished recording and coming up with enough copies on film for all sections. It meant staying up all night, but we did it.

The news coverage of the conference was extensive and favorable with my favorite reviewer in the *Saturday Review* who wrote "The White House Conference on Children was the biggest bar mitzvah on record."

Aside from wrapping up my work with the conference and handling one more encounter with a non-governmental bureaucracy, I finished my work for the White House Conference.

The Music Educators Conference had used a photograph of the charming young lady, Ruth McLain, on the front cover of their magazine. She called me quite excited with a request. She would like to get more copies for her relatives and friends, but the music educators said they had a rule that prohibited them from giving more than one copy to a person. After assuring her that we would straighten it out, I called the music educators who confirmed what they had told her. So, pulling the White House ploy again, I requested a dozen copies for the White House to be sent to me. Which I then sent off to the young lady in Hyndman, Kentucky.

With that, my duties with the White House Conference on Children were complete, and I handed over the duties for the White House Conference on Youth to Jim DenBoer who attended the snow bound meeting at Estes Park, Colorado.

Chapter Seven

The Blame Game

1971-1977

With my job at the White House Conference coming to an end, I would have to return to the position waiting for me in the Public Affairs office when another friend from our Social security days, Joe Preissig, came to my rescue. Joe, by this time, was working for the Bureau of Health Manpower. Dr. Ken Endicott, who had moved over from his position as director of the National Cancer Institute to lead the Health Manpower operation, was looking for someone to head its public information office. Joe suggested they look at me.

My meeting with Dr. Endicott was brief and very interesting. He offered me the job and said, "I'm hiring you because I think you'd be good at the job, So do it and come to me only if you need help." It took me a month or two before I came to believe that he meant what he said. His method of operating I found out was to hire people he thought could do the job well and stepped out of the way to be there only if they needed him.

The office I stepped into had not had a permanent director for many months. In addition to the acting director there was an information officer and two secretaries, Carol Miller from West Virginia and Florence Foelak with a lovely Brooklyn accent. Stew Hunter told me that whenever he called me, he hoped he would get her on the line so he could hear her Brooklyn accent. When I relayed that message to her, her answer was ," What accent!" What we didn't know at the time was that the two of us were going to have a long and very productive relationship.

Shortly after I came on board, Florence brought me a clipping from the *Cleveland Plain Dealer*. The reporter had called the Department information office with a question about medical education. That office referred her to the PHS. That office referred her to NIH. That office referred her to my office, which referred her to the medical education office which gave her the information she was seeking. But the article at hand wasn't about that information but was about her telephone voyage giving the names of the people, including mine, at each referral point. Carol and Florence both were annoyed because they had referred her to the right place and she wasn't very nice. After some argument, we agreed that in the future, we would give anyone who requested information that we did not have in hand the option of letting us get the information for them or letting them make the call themselves. With grumbling, that's what we did, and in the future that practice even yielded some very grateful callers.

We began receiving many letters from congressmen asking for help in responding to requests from their constituents demanding more support for nursing education. Since the nursing division was the proper place to handle them, I took a few of them down to Jessie Scott, the head of the division. When I asked her to answer them, she said she couldn't and admitted she had instigated the campaign. We then agreed that she would draft an answer, but I would send it out over my signature. I was learning fast.

One of the people I got to know and treasure was the Executive Officer, Bob Learmouth. He had been with Endicott at the Cancer Institute and in him I found another bureaucrat who believed in getting things done. We were to have a very close and long friendship. Dr. Endicott, when someone confronted him with an administrative problem, would often say, "Check that with Bob Learmouth. He's brighter than he looks."

Very early, I drafted speeches for Endicott. After the first outing, I asked him how things went. "I used every word," he said. It was several months later when I had a chance to be at a meeting where he gave one of my speeches. Any similarity between what I had written and what came out of his mouth was purely coincidental. When I confronted him and reminded him of his previous statement, he replied with a laugh, "Well I did, but just in a different order."

The job of the Bureau, which got its impetus from President Johnson's direction that the country needed 50,000 more doctors, was to support the schools of the health professions so they could turn out the needed health workers. The Bureau had four divisions: one for medical education, another for dental, one for nursing and the final one for the supporting health personnel.

With the passage of the Civil Rights Acts, there was a need to encourage more minorities to enter these professions. Before I came on board, Cliff Allen, a former army officer and POW in Korea, who now worked in our Office of Equal Opportunity, had contracted with a film company, Blackside, to make a motion picture to attract more minority candidates to medical schools. Now that I was here, he turned the project over to me. It was there that I was impressed with the professionalism and creativity of the president of the organization, Henry Hampton, and his sidekick, Tony Romas. The product, " Code Blue", was a fine motion picture that we made available to schools and organizations around the country.

We were to contract with them to make two more pictures in the years ahead. The first was one aimed at Hispanic audiences, and the other, produced in cooperation with the Robert Wood Johnson Foundation, was an exploration of "Innovations in Medical Education". It was with that film that I learned a couple of lessons.

After Henry and his crew put together the first rough cut, we decided to have a private showing with a group of officials from a number of medical associations to get their reaction and suggestions for the final product. Unfortunately we didn't emphasize before the showing that this, essentially, was a rough draft and we were asking for their input before it became final. When we opened the floor for comments, several of the participants tore into what they saw were the shortcomings. Even with the negative comments, we did pick up several useful suggestions, and I vowed never to make the same mistake again of exposing people unused to reviewing rough cuts for comments without briefing them extensively.

As we were filming one episode with the American Association of Medical Colleges (AAMC) at a location at a historic hotel in St. Petersburg, Florida, Henry noticed that the visible hotel help were all white. Behind the scenes, in the kitchen and laundry, the black help was hidden. When I returned to Washington, I wrote a letter to the Executive Officer of the AAMC and told him that meetings financed by the Federal Government should be held only at facilities that did not discriminate in employment. Several weeks later, I was attending an unrelated meeting at AAMC headquarters to take part in discussions about an upcoming conference when one of the participants mentioned in a tone that resembled a sneer that someone from the government had written actually telling them where they should hold meetings. After he finished, I said, "I wrote that letter." Deathly and embarrassing silence followed before we went on to another topic.

Henry, who for years was working on a documentary "Eyes on the Prize" about the civil rights movement, was rewarded with a nomination for an Oscar for the best documentary that year.

A few weeks after I was on the job, Duke Sybor showed up at the office seeing if there was any chance of a job opening. It must have taken me about three seconds before I gave him the job. It would be one of my better decisions, because he was a gift as a real professional with a sly sense of humor who would be with us for a number of years.

Morrie Turner the creator of the comic strip "Wee Pals", with whom I had become friendly at the White House Conference, came to Washington on some business, so Duke and I arranged to have lunch with him at a restaurant in the city's market area. I asked him if he would be willing to do a comic book that would encourage young minority boys and girls to consider health careers. He was only too willing, so I asked him how much he wanted for the job.

He thought for a moment and asked, "$50 a page and $100 for the cover?"

Both Duke and I said almost at the same moment, "What!"

He looked at us and asked, "Is that too much?"

"Morrie, that's not enough. Let's say $100 a page and $200 for the cover."

And we were in business, and it was the only time I had to argue with a contractor to raise his price. We supplied him with some background material, and in a very short time, we had the 24 page comic book on health careers for minority children.

At about this time, the Bureau was getting ready to give out a number of grants to the schools of the health professions. The extent and the number of grants seemed to us to be worth a public announcement, so with Duke drafting the news release, we put together a press package and sent the release up to the Department for approval and permission to hold a news conference to announce these major grants. After getting approval, we scheduled the news conference.

On the day of the conference, Duke, Florence and I went down to the HEW building with Dr. Endicott for the event only to be met with the HEW press officer who told us that the health advisor at the White House, a refugee from the PHS, had vetoed the news conference saying it was something that should be announced by the President. So, with the press arriving for the now unscheduled news conference and asking why it was not being held, I referred them to the Department press office and beat a retreat to our office at NIH.

Then the blame game started with the Department's press officer calling me and asking why we didn't realize it had to be cleared with the White House. I was having none of this and told him that was his job. Dr. Endicott asked me why it had happened, and I explained it to him and assured him that we had followed correct procedure but also that we could expect everyone involved to be running for the exit.

After that fiasco, we announced the grants in small batches and aimed the announcements at the local news outlets.

With the office running smoothly and Duke there, I had no compunction in accepting a request to join a White House task force that was set up to mollify Representative Barry Goldwater Jr., the son of the senator, who wanted the government to contract all their motion picture work to his Hollywood constituents. The task force was to investigate the possibility and to make recommendations. At the first meeting, I was assigned to lead the section that would see if contracting out all government work made sense.

Very soon it became obvious that the Defense Department dwarfed the rest of the government in film production with the Department of Agriculture a very distant second. To get a handle on the extent of the problem we prepared a questionnaire that would be sent to all government agencies. As we got the questionnaire into final shape, the Defense Department person in my section took me aside and told me that I wasn't asking the right questions. Expecting some unexpected help from him, I asked him what we should ask. His reply floored me. "I can't tell you."

With that helpful bit of advice, we sent out the questionnaire and sorted out the answers which were pretty much what we expected. It was then that I was introduced to Marjorie Greene who was on contract to help shepherd the whole enterprise. It was the start of another long time friendship. It was with her and the director of the project, Charles Joyce, that we visited several defense installations.

At the first one, Nellis Air Base in Southern California, we found a well equipped film studio which was used to produce a number of training films. As we checked the facilities, I noticed two 35mm film processing units--one still wrapped in plastic. When I asked why two and why was one not in use, we were told that was in case the first one broke down. We asked why they didn't contract with the film studios in nearby Hollywood, the colonel said they often were on a tight schedule. The log I perused showed that the machine had been used all of three times in the preceding year. We also were shown a fully equipped sound studio that was the same as one on the MGM lot that the commanding general had seen. Again, after reviewing the logs, we found it had been used very few times and generally for the general's talks to the troops.

Down at the Marine Corps El Toro Air Base near San Diego, we found a completely different story. They contracted out all their film processing to studios in Los Angeles. We asked what would happen if they needed overnight service, and they told us of the contract provision that called for overnight delivery in up to ten percent of their work if needed.

After I submitted my section's report recommending contracting out if it could be done economically and meeting all needed deadline deliveries, I returned to the bureau and never heard anything further about the recommendations.

Some time before this detail, I had seen a short animated film that had won the Academy Award as the best animated film of the year. It was produced by the Zagreb Film Studio in Yugoslavia which specialized in non-verbal animation. The title was "Ersatz" and was the story of a man who creates his entire environment by inflating patches of color. It was so clever and with a very subtle humor that the impression stayed with me for a long time. I began thinking that these creative people perhaps could help with our program of trying to reach some of our hard to reach groups.

I tried out the idea with Bob Learmouth who thought it was worth trying. There was a program known as Public Law 480 that was put in place after the war. During the war, the United States had loaned money and equipment to countries fighting the Nazis. Rather than requiring them to repay what could be large amounts causing economic hardship for them, we allowed the funds to stay in the country to be used by US agencies for projects that would benefit us. Yugoslavia was one of those countries. So we could use 480 money to have Zagreb film studio create a non-verbal animated film for our use.

We put in the request through proper channels and received approval to move ahead with the project. I phoned Zaga Anicic in Belgrade to tell her and have her help with our arrangements. I also spoke to a Mr. Zelimer Matko who was the director of the studio, and Bob and I were ready to start, but it was not to be. The morning of the day we were to leave, I was attending a staff meeting when Bob entered with a stricken look on his face. We went outside and he informed me that there was not enough 480 money left in Yugoslavia to start the project. As Robert Burns had written, "The best laid plans, etc. etc."

We didn't have too much time to mourn our disappointment when a reorganization took place which moved the Bureau of Health Manpower into an outfit called the Health Resources Administration. In addition to the Bureau, we would now be saying prayers over the Bureau of Health Services Research and the National Center for Health Statistics. Our sister organization, the Health Services Administration, was located in the Parklawn building in suburban Maryland, where we had to move.

About the time of the reorganization, Casper Weinberger, Secretary of HEW, issued an edict that required all agencies to reduce the size of their public information staff. There were 102 who were in that category in our new agency. By moving positions around, I was able to consolidate our public information staff to 32 which satisfied the edict.

But our sister agency, HSA, to cut back to the required number, planned to eliminate the journal *Public Health Reports* with its staff of four. That prestigious journal was entering its 100th year. I went to Endicott and asked if we could take it over to continue its legacy, and he agreed. So, the editor, Marion Tebbens and her staff, would continue to report on public health matters. Since it was to celebrate its centennial, they selected one significant article from its archives for each issue.

One other issue came up with HSA. Their public information officer was an extremely bright and talented man who had one annoying characteristic. Ted Cron knew when he was right even if his boss didn't agree, and Ted would never let go if he knew that he and not the boss was following the correct procedure. This, over the years, led to his being moved from his job by the annoyed bosses. And so it was now. Dr. Van Zant, the deputy director of HSA called and asked me if we would take Ted, and they would give us the position and funds. With Endicott's blessing, I agreed, and Ted came on board.

It was about a year later when Van Zant asked Dr. Endicott, since it had been a year, to give them back the position and the funds. Endicott agreed. When he told me, I shot back, "That's not what we agreed!" So I phoned Van Zant who, they said, "was not in." Receiving no call back, I tried several times to speak to him each time being told he was no available. It was then that I got the message that the cowardly bureaucrat did not want to be confronted by me.

With our country's bicentennial coming up, Ted and I thought it would make sense to produce a book recounting our nation's history in the field of public health. It was a great job in which he could use his talents, and he plunged right in to the job, and produced a beautifully written and designed volume.

Meanwhile, Marion Tebbens and her staff were grinding out issue after issue of Public Health Report's centennial year with reprints of important articles from its archives including historic ones like "The Etiology of Pellagra" and "Sulfanilamide in the Treatment of Leprosy." She came to me with a question about a major manuscript that had been submitted to her. It was a projection of where health care costs in the US were headed in the years ahead. The researchers conclusion that health care costs in the country would reach 12 percent of GNP and the economic costs of illness would amount to two trillion dollars by the year 2,000. Being very short sighted, I thought the researchers had to be way off, but Marion said she had checked with some statisticians who gave the analysis good marks. The public debate following the article's appearance and the subsequent actual increase in our nation's health costs reaffirmed Marion's judgment and my lack of it.

One of the programs with which I was now involved was those of the National Center for Health Statistics which conducted with the Office of Census a Health Interview Survey where census takers actually went out and conducted studies with a carefully selected sample of the nation's population. The results were important indicators of the state of the nation's health and gave useful hints of where more effort would be needed. In recent years, it had been getting more difficult to get respondents to cooperate with the survey. The people who were conducting the study asked for our help.

In reviewing the material that was being sent to induce people to take part in the survey, I thought that the letters asking for cooperation were a little too formal and bureaucratic, so I turned to Bob Sampson with whom we worked in the water pollution program. Bob had been the direct mail expert with the J Walter Thompson advertising agency. He reviewed the material and drafted a host of letters to induce citizens to take part in the survey.

After receiving his proposed letters, I passed them on to the statistics people and on to the Census Bureau. A short time later, we received an answer from them turning down Bob's efforts saying, "They're not like government letters." When the Center's people passed this on to me, I urged them to insist on using them. Finally, the Census Bureau made an offer. They would use them but only in a controlled test comparing the response rates between the two sets of letters. We couldn't ask for anything better, and when the results came in, it was obvious that the letters that Bob had produced also produced much greater response and participation than the former ones.

A short time after this, the Center for Health Statistics was about to release a report on height variations between racial groups in the United States. It showed that blacks were growing at a faster rate than their white counterparts. Duke Sybor, working with Jim Walker, our graphic designer, developed life-sized silhouette figures to be used at a news conference announcing these findings. It turned out to be a very cheerful and informative press outing.

A group of academics, fulfilling requirements of a grant they had received, submitted a manuscript on the effect of medical economics and the delivery of health care. I turned it over to Ted Cron for editing, and he did what any good editor would do: he turned the dense and academic prose into readable copy. When we sent the revised text to the grantees, the howls were heard loud and clear. Dr. Endicott asked me to handle the hurt and outraged professors. I toned down some of Ted's editing enough to placate the academics, but Ted protesting showed me one paragraph which we agreed should be preserved for posterity. We enlarged and framed it so it could be hung on the wall in my office.

"Since it has been axiomatic in regionalization theory that in the increasingly specialized, high technology arena of medical care, the reorganization of resources to correct imbalances of distribution and the replacement of institutional atomization with structural linkages are necessary conditions for the production of quality services, the extent to which such perceptions have informed these programs or conversely the lessons of their experiences for subsequent health policy are of no small interest."

From time to time, someone who came into my office would look at this sentence of academic gibberish and nod knowingly as if they understood the meaning.

Although my plans using PL480 money in Yugoslavia had been thwarted previously, I hadn't given up the idea of using the talented people of the Zagreb Film Studio. Chatting one day with Ken Endicott, I broached the subject again. This time perhaps we could contract with the World Health Organization (WHO) to be our middleman in a project to make a non-verbal animated film on some health topic and then market test it across cultural and linguistic lines. He agreed that I could go ahead but expressed some well founded doubts about working with that organization.

So, once again, I spoke to Zelimer Matko at the Zagreb Film group, and through the proper channels asked the World Health Organization if they would like to work with us under contract to develop a non-verbal animated film on a health topic that then would be tested across national and language lines. The reply was rapid and affirmative, so I travelled to Geneva to meet with the WHO officials who would run the project.

The first meeting was pleasant and affirmative but, if I had been more aware, a hint of what was to come, I would have been uneasy. The gentleman who would be in charge of WHO's end of the project pushed to make the arrangement a grant rather than a contract. I declined and we moved on. Although I initially thought the project should be about family planning, another person made a much better suggestion. She suggested that the film should be about vaccination. It was also agreed that the film maker would be encouraged to use its creativity to go ahead with the project.

And it was set. At least I thought it was until I received a report from WHO that they had sent out a proposal to a number of possible agents along with a pedestrian story board that had been put together by someone at WHO. Since this violated our agreement to use the creativity of the film maker, I promptly cancelled the contract. And, oh what a fuss there was!

Our Office of International Health (OIH) demanded a meeting, but before going, I discussed it with Dr. Endicott and had his assurance that he would back me up. With that assurance, I went to the meeting where I was confronted by what seemed to be the whole staff. Paul Ehrlich, the head of the office, informed me that I could not cancel the contract, because the OIH had so many projects with WHO. I carefully explained why I had cancelled the contract and told them that my decision was final.

Then they offered to send me to Geneva to work it out: an offer I declined and told them if WHO wished to negotiate, they could come here, and that's what happened. The first thing the WHO representative said to me as we sat down to discuss why I had cancelled the contract was that they had selected the Zagreb Film Studio for the project. I carefully explained that, although I was pleased that they had finally made a selection, that was not the reason the contract was cancelled. I explained as clearly as I could that their pedestrian storyboard was a clear violation of our agreement and it dealt a blow at the ability of the Zagreb people to use their creativity.

After some dancing around the issue, we agreed that I would go to Zagreb and ask them to disregard the storyboard so that they could use their own creativity in coming up with a more acceptable product. It was on this trip that I was able to observe State Department bureaucracy at its worst. Since I was routed through our embassy in Belgrade to have my travel in Yugoslavia arranged, I encountered two Yugoslav women workers there. They were trying to get my travel arranged which required certification by an American employee who was not responding, but they were not allowed to enter the area where that employee sat.

The two women were desperately trying to get my travel certified getting little cooperation from the cloistered American office, one turned to me and asked, " Why are you so calm?

"Do you want me to get annoyed at you?"

At almost the last moment when I could make my train, the certification came through. I thanked the two women, noting their names, and when I got back to my office sent a letter to the ambassador complimenting them on their concern and efficiency. That Christmas, I received a surprise greeting card from one of them.

The next day I met with Matko and explained to him what had happened. I acknowledged that it might be difficult, but would they disregard the storyboard and come at the project as if they were starting from scratch. He said they would try, but it really was a useless exercise. They touched it up a little, but the final product emerged pretty much as the WHO product. What I learned from that exercise was not to rely on verbal agreements but put them in writing.

The work in the office was going on well. We had organized the operation in three sections: the first was the press operation headed by Duke Sybor, then there was the technical publication section with Marion Tebben, and finally there was the graphic design office with Jim Walker who had come with us from the Bureau of Health Manpower. Florence Foelak, who was a genius at handling details and who never hesitated to tell me when she thought I was wrong, was my administrative aide.

Our organization had a visitor from England. Dr. Malcolm Forsythe, the medical director with the Kent Area Office of England's National Health Service (NHS). In chatting with him and with everything in place in the office, I began to think of taking advantage of a program that probably had been designed for the scientific community. It was a work-study program that would allow me to work in another country studying at close hand that country's health care system. So I checked with Dr. Endicott to see if I could study how the public obtained its information about the provisions of the NHS. With his OK, I submitted the proposal to spend six months on this project.

Eventually, the project was approved, and after some pleas to Dr. Forsythe, he convinced the other officers at the Area Office that they could accommodate me without disrupting their routine. But before we could leave on this project, two events took place that might have derailed it. The first was the election of Jimmy Carter as president and the appointment of Joseph Califano as Secretary of HEW. Shortly after taking over, he proceeded to dismiss almost all agency heads so that he could put his choices in place which meant that Endicott was no longer my boss. Until a new agency head could be put in place, Dr. Harold Margolies would be it. Luckily he had no objection to my project.

The other event came on us suddenly as we were preparing to leave. As happens from time to time, the Congress was not able to come up with the funding of the government, so all travel was cancelled. I called Malcolm to explain the delay, and two days later, Charles Miller phoned me and said, "Get out of town fast." Congress had approved a short term budget.

It didn't take Eileen and my daughter Sarah who would spend several months with us in England long to grab our luggage and go on what would be some of the most rewarding months of our lives.

Chapter Eight
Our English Adventure
1977-1978

The first few days, we stayed at a small hotel in Bayswater and did a little exploring while our body clocks became used to the British time. I spoke with Malcolm who arranged for us to be picked up by the Area's driver, a former rural policeman with whom I was to have many extremely interesting talks in the months ahead. We had come prepared to suffer through a British winter but were faced with an unusual hot spell when we arrived in October.

The driver drove us from our London hotel down to our new digs in the Matron's Flat at the cottage hospital in Sevenoaks, Kent. A cottage hospital, we learned, was one that was run by doctors who were general practitioners . The hospital itself stood high on a hill overlooking the railway station at the section of the town called Tubs Hill. Sevenoaks itself was, we were to find, a pleasant commuters' paradise only a 33 minute train ride from Charing Cross Station in London. The town was located on high ground overlooking the North Downs, and had grown up in the 13th, 14th and 15th centuries. The grammar school, which was founded in 1418 by Sir. William Sevenoaks, was still in operation.

Nearby was the magnificent manor house with surrounding grounds known as Knole Park which had been passed from Cardinal Cramner to Henry the Eighth when the king let it be known that he would be willing to accept it as a gift. We were to spend many lovely days exploring those precincts. On our first weekend in Sevenoaks, we went for a stroll through the village and over to Knole House. As we entered the precincts, we saw a few beautiful deer grazing over at some woods and tried to be as quiet as possible so as not to disturb them. As we walked over a rise, we were confronted by the spectacular sight of the mansion and hundreds of deer. As soon as they saw us, several came over to see what goodies we had brought for them. we laughed at how quiet we thought we would have to be so as not to disturb them. This was just the first of our many visits to the lovely mansion and its grounds.

Our flat itself consisted of a large living-dining room, a bedroom, kitchen and bathroom with a glorious deep bath tub that would be a delightful warm refuge during the cold English winters. Our daughter, Sarah. had her bedroom across the hall. The monthly rent was 30 pounds.

Malcolm phoned to make sure we were settling in and made a date to pick me up the following Monday to drive me to what would be my new office with the Kent Area Health Authority in the town of Maidstone where I met the staff with whom I was going to become very familiar in the months ahead. Peter La Fleming was the Executive Officer. In addition there was a nursing officer, Eileen Haig, and the financial manager, Basil Spencer. All decisions for administering the NHS programs in the area were made by their consensus. In addition, I was introduced to Dr. Gillian Mathews and Eric Byers both of whom became very dear friends.

The next day, I rented a car and drove to Maidstone on my own. As I entered the first roundabout I encountered, I dutifully went into it turning to the right. It took me just one terrified moment as a lorry came at me to realize that I was now in England where you drove on the left hand side of the road. Luckily, I never made that mistake again.

I had come expecting to explore how people in Britain obtained their information about their health care under the NHS and quickly became aware of organizations attached to the more than 200 districts of the NHS which were called Community Health Councils (CHC) They were in their fourth year of existence in 1978, the year we were there. These consumer organizations were legislated by the NHS Reorganization Legislation in 1974.

It was through these Councils that the views of the community were to be presented to the administrators of the health service so that those Councils could become more responsive to the needs of the consumers. At least that was the theory. In practice, I was to find, that depended so much on the whims and wishes of the administrators.

A book that was recommended to me was *The Reorganised National Health Service* by Ruth Levitt who now was editor of the *CHC NEWS*. This excellently written book opened the door to my understanding of the history of the NHS reorganization and the problems faced by these newly organized CHCs. I didn't hesitate to call her and arrange a meeting. When I arrived at her office, I was met by a young and very attractive slim woman with long hair who, I assumed with my pre-conceived idea, was Ruth Levitt's secretary. So, when Ruth introduced herself to me, I must have been smiling thinking of how wrong I had been.

In the days ahead, she helped me immensely to understand the programs and the obstacles faced by these consumer organizations. In her position as editor of the *CHC NEWS*, she had one of the best pedestals from which to observe how the CHCs were getting underway, and also to suggest ways for me to meet the CHC members who would further my understanding.

While I was getting underway with my project, Eileen and Sarah were exploring what Sevenoaks had to offer. Eileen experienced something that could only have happened in a small town in rural England. One day, she was shopping at the market in the town, but when she came back to the flat, she realized that the bottle of wine she had bought had been left on the counter when she checked out. A few days later, when she was shopping there again, she mentioned about her forgotten wine to the clerk at the checkout counter. He said, "Oh, you're the one who left this here" and retrieved the bottle of wine from under the counter and handed it to her.

One other experience was a chance meeting with Ed Greene, Marjorie's husband on the London Underground. Eileen and I had made arrangements to meet at a church in Trafalgar Square for dinner that night. I finished some business in Maidstone, and caught a train to London which broke down outside of Sevenoaks. Now, rushing to get to London and meet Eileen and Sarah, I caught another train into Sevenoaks and transferred to a London express. When it arrived at an unfamiliar Cannon Street station in London, I grabbed an underground Circle Line train in the direction of Charing Cross. As I was going for a seat, someone, who turned out to be Ed Greene, tapped me saying, "Mort? Mort Lebow?" They had just moved to

London where he was working for First Chicago Bank. So, quickly exchanging phone numbers, we reestablished contact that we had lost several months before.

Then two events changed my mind about how "socialized medicine" was working in Britain. I came there with some preconceived ideas of how their system worked. Then I heard about the granddaughter of the matron at Sevenoaks hospital, a child of eight or nine years old, suddenly developed double vision. Her GP, realizing that the case was beyond his capabilities, referred her to a neurosurgeon at Guys Hospital in London. That consultant (specialist in our vocabulary) found that she had a fast growing but non-malignant childhood tumor in her brain. What followed was an operation to remove the tumor, complete post operation care, rehabilitation and referral to social services for home schooling and medical follow-up. All of this without that driving fear of how they were going to pay for all of this.

The other event was a meeting Malcolm arranged for me with a young GP who had established his practice in rural Kent. He was living and conducting his practice from the former home of one of the Rolls Royce partners. He had first come to the community for a cricket game and was so taken with the local area that he decided to start a practice there. As we discussed his practice and the NHS, I asked him how he would feel about a fee for service plan as we had in the US. He shook his head and said, "I can't imagine practicing where I had to decide whether my patients could afford their treatments."

As I tried to understand how the public and the management of the NHS were interacting, I began to understand the important distinctions between how the British system and ours were formed and operated. When the NHS was first brought forth shortly after the war by the Labour government, it was an attempt to deliver health services when and where they were needed at no immediate cost to the patient. In contrast, when the US entering upon a health care system, the immediate question was "How are we going to pay for it?" Two different questions which led to two very different systems. Time and time again in my discussions with people about how the NHS worked, it was referred to as "free" care, and I eventually would point out that it wasn't free but paid for with taxes.

One of the first CHCs I visited was in Medford on the South side of the Thames. It was there in the board room of the 900 year old hospital that I sat in on their board meeting. My hosts complained about the bad acoustics, but I was much more fascinated by the fact that I was sitting in the same room that Dickens had described when Oliver Twist stood before the Beadle and asked, "Can I have some more please?"

As word got out about my presence on the scene and what I was trying to do, I began receiving invitations to talk with various organizations about my work. On one occasion, at the Wandsworth CHC, I was asked to give my impressions of our two different health care systems. It was the first time I really had to put this comparison into words. I started by pointing out that the British system provided basic health care to 90 percent of the population at no immediate costs to the patients, and in that respect the NHS provided better access to care than in the US. But there were elements in the British system that would not live up to our system.

First of all, there was the question of queues for non-emergency care. It was a weakness in the system of which they were too aware. Then there was question of technology. As an example, Britain, with a population of one third that of the US had but 12 CAT scanning devices in the whole British Isles in spite of the fact that those were developed by EMI a British Company while in the US, there were more than 560. And finally, there was a disconnect between the GP and the Consultant. Once the GP referred the patient, the Consultant was under no obligation to send the results of the patient's care back to the GP, although, in many cases the consultant did so.

As far as the queues were concerned, I was aware of how many people would skip the queues. If a person needed a hip replacement and was to wait a year for a scheduled operation under the NHS, he or she could then ask the orthopedic surgeon about going private. Then the Consultant would take out his book for the private patients and schedule it for a convenient time for both of them, because under the inducements to get the Consultants to remain in the NHS, the government allowed them to practice up to two half days for their private practice. I knew just from the cottage hospital in Sevenoaks that a well known orthopedic surgeon from Guys hospital would motor out once a week and pay to use the two operating rooms to perform his private procedures for people who could afford to skip the queues.

Another invitation I received was from the planning group at St. Thomas Hospital across the Thames from Westminster and Big Ben. They were curious about how the Health Planning Act was working out in the US. It was designed, as I explained to them to encourage Health Systems Agencies serving populations of between 500,000 and one million people to plan for the delivery of health services. As the questioning proceeded about how effective the Act was, I acknowledged that political pressure was always present and compared it to what could be happening at St. Thomas. I said, "Look, if you wanted to have a new heart unit and the Region turned you down, your people would get in touch with your MP, and he would clear the way for approval." It was as if I had touched a raw nerve, because one of the planning group said, "Malcolm has been speaking out of turn." I assured them that he hadn't, but I was just talking about political realities.

We were really suffering through the unusual hot spell with our winter cloths when we travelled up to Edinburgh, Scotland where I was to meet a fellow named David Player who was the head of the Scottish Health Education Council. We had planned to arrive on a Friday night so we would have the weekend to explore Edinburgh, and when we arrived we were greeted by a cold and wet night which is what we dressed for when we left Washington. The next day, November 11, was bright and sunny and viciously cold, but we were treated to their Armistice Day parade at the Castle Walk. From that day on, we lived in the British winter for which we had planned.

Dr. David Player turned out to be a delight and became another lifelong friend. A former GP and a dedicated socialist, he was in the midst of a campaign to educate the public about the risks of tobacco smoking. He also would become a campaigner to try to come up with solutions to the homeless problems first in Scotland and later when he became head of the British Health Education Council. It was there, years later during the

Thatcher government that he completed a study called "The Widening Divide" showing the difference between access to health care for well to do and the poorer populations. He was told not to issue a press release, so obeying that instruction, he didn't. But he did hold a press conference. It was the next day that Thatcher dissolved the Council and brought it back as the Health Education District. Although he applied for the Director's job, he knew he wasn't going to get it.

Following a suggestion from Ruth Leavitt, I visited Tom Richardson, a former labor leader, who was now secretary of the Oxfordshire CHC. He explained how difficult it was to get the professionals to listen to the comments from the CHC when those comments were complaints about the service being provided by the health system. It was a complaint I began hearing from time to time as I began seeing a division of opinion between those who were supposed to represent the public and those professionals who were actually running the system.

While we were in Oxford, Tom urged me to meet Jane Robinson who was the chairperson of a group called the Citizens Association. Jane was the driving force behind that organization. Although it was small, with no more than 1,000 members, it achieved a notoriety completely out of its size or resources in the cause of patients' rights and was well informed about the working of the health system. Jane explained that they placed emphasis on pursuing complaints patients may have against the system or against individual practitioners.

Tom also introduced me to someone who was doing some very interesting work and would cross paths with me some years later after I left government service. Dr. Iain Chalmers at Oxford University was leading an effort to put together in usable form all the controlled scientific studies having to do with women's health. When he completed the study, anyone could see if any single procedure would be of benefit or not.

And finally, Tom told me of a meeting that was scheduled at the University of Leeds where a number of executives from CHCs would be meeting to discuss their achievements and problems. He arranged for me to attend where I was to get a fairly broad view of the progress the CHCs were making in becoming the voice of the public.

It was there that I met Jack Hallas, author of *CHCs In Action*, who described in great detail how CHCs, primarily in Yorkshire, were faring in their formative years. Also at the meeting was Leslie Rosen, chairman of the Leeds Eastern CHC, who brought his experience with the Trade Union movement with him when he was nominated for the job by the Leeds City Council.

It was on my return to London from Leeds that Eileen and I experienced one of the most exhilarating theatre experiences of our stay. We had bought tickets to "Macbeth" at the Young Vic theatre on the South Bank. I met Eileen at Waterloo Station where we grabbed a bite and headed the two blocks to the theatre, a very uncomfortable venue, where we found that the play was to be presented without an intermission. The two leads, of whom we had never heard, were Ian McCellen and Judi Dench. Gritting our teeth, we seated ourselves and were blown away by the incredible performance not only by the leads but by the entire cast. We left to catch the train back to Sevenoaks walking on air.

From time to time, visitors from the States came by to bring us news of what was going on back there. Jon Spivak, correspondent for *The Wall Street Journal* had been reassigned to London to cover the news from there. He got in touch with me, and we had several meetings including a trip down to Kent where I tried to show him some lovely parts of the Kentish countryside, but Jon was always more interested in the workings of the NHS. As far as possible, I tried to help him out.

The visit that caused the most concern at the office was the announcement that Secretary Califano, on his European trip, was going to visit the Kent Area Health Authority. Malcolm asked me to meet with the Executive Committee to tell them anything to help them prepare for the meeting. I had heard a rumor that Califano was considering a run for the US Senate from New York, so, with this in mind, I advised the group of four that they should be fairly relaxed since the meeting was probably put on his schedule to enhance his resume. When he arrived with his entourage, it included John Blamphim who I knew very well since he was the public information officer for the PHS. We had a chance to chat, and I filled him in as best I could with how the NHS was operating here in Kent.

Some time after that visit, I received a request from Dr. Margolies to get whatever information I could about the hospice movement in Britain that would help as they planned to introduce legislation for hospice programs in the US. Dame Cicely Saunders, a British physician, introduced the concept of hospice care for the dying at St. Christopher's Hospital in a suburb of London. So Eileen and I drove over to St. Christopher's on one of the infrequent sunny days that winter. As we drove up to the entrance of the hospice, we immediately noticed something different. There were children getting out of their parents' cars and running into the building. This indeed was going to be different.

After parking our car, we went into the hospice and sought out the main office. I explained what I was there for and, in very short order, received a mass of information which I packed up and mailed back to the US. Whether that material ever found its way into consideration for the legislation that eventually emerged I had no idea.

Florence had kept me up to date on what was going on in the information office back in the States with regular letters and phone calls. One day, she said she would like to come over for a visit to see what I had been doing and to be a tourist. So we set a date, and I was able to get a flat for her in Hampstead that a friend of mine, Graham Benson, had available for a reasonable 40 pound fee. When she arrived, I took her to the flat and made plans to see her that evening when Eileen would come to London and we would go to the London National Opera after a meal at our favorite Italian restaurant.

She brought with her notes from Duke and other memos bringing me up to date on what was going on back in my office. The first weekend, she came down to Sevenoaks, and we were able to show her the village and Knole House. Then we drove through the Kent countryside down to the seaside town of Rye where we had dinner in a pub that had a sign painted on its wall, "Restored 1402 AD." After a week during which she and Eileen visited Brighton and hopped over to Paris for a short visit, she explored other tourist spots in England. She departed with my best wishes to our Washington crew.

While we were enjoying our stay in England, Califano gave the Health Resources Administration a new administrator, Henry "Hank" Foley. As he looked around at his staff, he, of course, noticed my absence and began making noises that he should recall me. When Duke heard these rumblings, he called and passed the information on to me with the wise words of advice, "Make yourself unavailable." Fortunately wiser voices prevailed, and I was allowed to finish my study. But Duke also passed on a rumor that I was going to be moving on as the Public Information Officer in the Surgeon General's office. I told him, honestly, that it was news to me. Whether he believed me or not, I didn't know.

Malcolm suggested that I go to Winchester to meet a fellow named Ian Dillow who was the public information officer for the Wessex Regional Health Authority. Eileen and I took a train down to Winchester a day early so that we could explore the town and its famous cathedral. As we were wandering through that magnificent structure and looking up at the faraway ceilings, we heard a voice saying, "Look down! Look down!" There was an older man who was pointing to a mirror on a stand, so we complied with his direction and saw in much greater detail, the magnificent design in the ceiling. He then took us in hand and gave us a tour of the place that we would not have noticed on our own.

When we offered to take him out for a drink, he demurred and went on his way.

The next day, I met with Ian in his office and received a detailed education on the public information program in the Wessex Region. And, as with so many other people we met in our sojourn in Britain, we had another long term friend.

One of the practices in Britain that was at odds with those we had in the US was the issue of how they dealt with the malpractice of doctors. In essence, they did not. For in the year preceding our visit, there had only been twelve suits successfully brought against NHS physicians. When I met with a gentleman from Britain's legal aide division, I couldn't help commenting that those twelve suits would not constitute enough to support one legal practice in our country. He then explained the complex legal machinery a person would have to navigate before even bringing a suit to court. I thought there should be some way to bridge the gulf between the British restrictive climate and our runaway system.

A few weeks before Christmas, Eileen saw that the Juilliard String Quartet was to give a program of Mozart quartets at the Queen Elizabeth Hall on the South Bank. Since we had lost touch with Joel Krosnick, the cellist for the Quartet, we thought it would be a good chance to catch up with him. And my, what an experience we had! From the moment the quartet started on the first Mozart quartet, there was a magical and thrilling feeling in that hall. The tension just kept building until after the last quartet of the day finished, the staid British audience just erupted with cheering and applause. Of course, after the concert, we made our way backstage to catch up with Joel and start a long relationship with the Quartet.

As Christmas approached, we made arrangements at the flat to accommodate our two other children and our son's friend, Rob. Rob arrived at Heathrow right on schedule, but Edward and Ellen had to be diverted to Amsterdam because of the first day of dense fog. After a chaotic next day, I picked them up at Victoria Station and we all got together at our digs at Sevenoaks. Because of the fire regulations, no candles or electric lights were permitted on our tree, so the arts majors exhibited their prowess in making paper decorations which we use to this day.

We arranged through a friend at Her Majesty's Printing Office for the children to visit the installation at the House of Lords. We found out later that the staff was gritting their teeth at the prospect of entertaining a group of children but were pleasantly surprised by this group of inquisitive and knowledge people including two art majors. Our children were all so impressed with the restoration of old manuscripts that was underway at that office.

After Edward and Rob left for the States, Ellen stayed on for several weeks. The day before she was to leave, I had an appointment with the staff of the Brighton CHC, so we all motored down. They went off sightseeing while I met with the Brighton CHC folks. As we were driving back to Sevenoaks, Ellen observed that this was only the second day in the month she had been in Britain that the sun had shined all day. Then we realized that Eileen and I had really become acclimated, because it had made no impression on us.

Early in the new year, I received an invitation to give a talk to a class of public health students at the University of Louvain in Belgium. Dr. Jon Blampan, whom I had met in Washington, extended the invitation which I grabbed immediately. Eileen and I flew to Brussels and had a day to sightsee before I was scheduled to give my talk. on Malcolm's recommendation, we took a train to Brugges which might well have been labeled, the Chocolate Capital of Belgium. As we got off the train we witnessed the police very efficiently separating the two sets of soccer fans who were descending on the town for a match.

So, after spending a lovely day in Brugges, we returned to Brussels for some more sightseeing. It was there, on Brussels' cobblestone streets, that Eileen twisted her ankle badly. We grabbed a cab to the train station and made our way to our hotel in Louvain. I called Dr. Blampan who recommended ice on the ankle with a promise to pick us up the next day. It was then that he guided us through the hospital and past lines of waiting patients as Eileen was examined and x-rayed. It was with great relief that we heard nothing was broken. Jon said that I might receive a bill for the treatment, but it never arrived.

Then, while Eileen rested, Jon introduced me to his class of public health students who subjected me to a very intense and intelligent grilling about our public health programs in the US especially our anti-smoking public information efforts. I was surprised to have to defend our efforts to tell people how to conduct their lives by urging them not to smoke. After the really stimulating experience, Jon took us to lunch at the faculty club which was in a carefully restored old barn where we had, what turned out to be, one of the best meals we had in Europe.

Back in England, we arranged a visit for my mother who quickly became fascinated by the lovely landscape in Kent and the lambs who butted their heads in greetings. Shortly after, my brother with some of his friends visited, and we became ready and a little reluctant to leave and come home. We extended our stay for a few weeks to attend the wedding of our friends, the Bensons, and then our stay was coming to an end.

As we packed and cleared up loose ends, I found that Florence, with great foresight, had arranged for us to have an allowance for extra baggage on our flight home. I also began to put my thoughts together about what I found in my study of the CHCs.

The effectiveness of the CHCs depended on two things. The first, and probably most important, was the effectiveness of the secretary of the CHC. If he or she came from a background in labor or local government, the CHC was more active in representing the public needs before the NHS. If, on the other hand, the secretary had been appointed by the Area or local authorities without these backgrounds, the CHC would become an adjunct to the wishes of the NHS management team. Generally, those CHCs in urban areas like Central London, Liverpool, Leeds etc. were much more likely to be active and pushing the NHS management on behalf of the public. If, on the other hand, with some exceptions, the CHCs in the more rural areas tended to follow the leads of the management.

There was one other trend of which I became aware. and that was the affinity of the CHCs efforts to come close to the desires of the General Practitioners. Although the GPs made out well under the NHS, their closeness with the needs of their patients often mirrored the thrust of the CHC. I thought that it was likely that the two would join forces in the near future, and this turned out to be partially right when, a few years later on a visit to Britain, I was invited to the annual meeting of the Association CHCs in York where a representative of the National Association of General Practitioners suggested a closer link with the work of the CHCs.

As we left Britain, I was thinking of how I could summarize my experiences and did that with a rather long paper entitled, "The Child Learns to Walk: A Look at Community Health Councils in their Fourth Year."

So this ended an exciting seven months which we savored for years.

Chapter Nine

Supervisor of the Year

1978-1979

We had the weekend to settle in. On Monday, Florence came by to drive me to the office. As we pulled away from our house, I became panicked thinking she was driving on the wrong side of the road. It took me just a moment for it to sink in that I was back where people drove on the right, or correct, side of the road.

After I made the appropriate greetings to my staff, I strolled over to Hank Foley's office to introduce myself. As I stood in the doorway to his office, he looked up questioningly until I introduced myself. We chatted for a brief time never alluding to the fact that I knew he had considered ordering me back from Britain before my project was completed.

One of the first projects I considered starting was to take a leaf from Ruth Levitt's book and to start a newsletter for our Health Planning Agencies that would help them exchange ideas and give them an opportunity to let the others know where they were succeeding in implementing their planning for health care delivery in their areas. Within our bureaucracy, things weren't as simple as I had seen in Britain. First I had to submit a proposal to the White House Budget Office through the proper channels. This, of course, didn't happen overnight, but eventually when approval did come through, I was able to hire someone to gather material from the Health Planning Agencies to get the newsletter started.

With that underway, we received a visit from a young woman, Melba Meader, a former high school English teacher who had just become a White House Management Intern. She was interviewing a number of office directors to see which office she would select as a home during her year as an intern. I was amused at why she was even talking to me and asked her why she was even here, because, as I told her, she really should be looking for a spot in an office that was more in line with her needs as a management person. After she listened politely and departed, I thought I had seen the last of her and got down to public information business. Several days later, after she had made the rounds of our agency, she showed up and informed me that she would like to set up in our office. To say I was surprised would be putting it mildly, but I asked Florence to help Melba get settled.

Among other things, Florence asked her what kind of typewriter she wanted. Melba replied that she didn't need one to which Florence said, "Everyone in this office uses a typewriter." And so we had another employee. Sometime later I asked her why she had chosen our office, and she said, "You were the only one to try to talk me out of coming on."

Since she was a management intern, I called Charlie Miller who was deputy in the Department's Budget Office and asked him if he would take her on. He checked with the Director of the office and told her to come ahead. It was there that she was immersed in the details of the Department's budget process. After a time, I suggested that she might want to get some experience on the Hill to see close up how the legislative process worked. And that's what she did.

So while she was getting the experience that she would need in her career, Hank Foley saw that we were not getting use of her at HRA. He called me in and asked why I was not using her in our agency. I explained that as a White House Management Intern, she really needed as broad an experience as possible. He wasn't happy about it, but there wasn't too much we could do to pull her back.

It was getting to the time when distinguished service awards were to be handed out, and I was surprised to find that Duke and others had put me in for the award of "Supervisor of the Year." I was amazed and a little honored until I read the write up that I'm sure Duke had a hand in, because it gave me the award as a supervisor who had been absent for more than half a year, and the office had operated well without me. At the awards ceremony, I joked that I wondered what awards I would have gotten if I had stayed away for a whole year.

There wasn't too much time to savor that award when I was faced with another problem. A young woman who worked for Alice Haywood, the Public Information Officer for the Center for Health Statistics had brought a civil rights complaint against her saying that because of her race she wasn't being allowed to get significant assignments.

As a possible settlement, she agreed to drop her complaint if she could be transferred to my office. I talked it over with Alice and agreed to the transfer. When she came to me for an interview, I told her that she would work in the press office reporting to Duke Sybor. He would discuss her assignments and they could work out the details. Luckily, Duke sat down with her, and they worked out a plan with a list of products to be delivered with the appropriate due dates. When the two of them agreed, they both signed the document.

Within a very short time, the young woman filed a complaint against me only this time she filed a legal complaint in court. It was just about this time that some of her assignments were coming due. As the dates approached, and she was incapable of completing the assignments, she abruptly resigned from government, and we did not hear from her again. Although Alice and I were glad that episode was over, I was sad that such an important safeguard against discrimination was being misused by an incompetent person.

The rumor that Duke had asked me about while I was in Britain concerning my taking a job in the Surgeon General's office turned out to have some truth in it. Charlie Miller asked me to come down and be interviewed by Dr. Julius Richmond who was the Assistant Secretary for Health as well as the US Surgeon General. Before I would agree, I spoke to the man who was holding down that spot and told him I would not do the interview if it meant stepping over him. He assured me that he wanted to be relieved, so I agreed to the interview.

The interview went well, and Dr. Richmond offered me the job. All that was needed now was a sign off by the Secretary's office. Much to my surprise, they refused to accept me. I thought that would be the final words, but Dr. Richmond dug in his heels saying that he should be the judge of who would be on his staff. This standoff went on for a few weeks until it was decided that I would meet with Secretary Califano's headhunter. It was an orderly meeting as he explained it was no reflection on my qualifications, but the Secretary wanted a woman or a minority in that position. When I heard that. I said, "Would it help if I came in drag?" With both of us laughing, the meeting ended, and I assumed that was also the end of the whole affair, but strange things were happening that would reverse the impasse.

President Carter decided that he wanted to remove the education programs from the Department and establish a cabinet level Department of Education. Secretary Califano was opposed to the idea and was working behind the President's back to sabotage the effort in Congress. Since it is almost impossible to keep a secret in Washington, the President found out and fired Califano. With that, Dr. Richmond requested that I report to his office as the Director of Public Information. I asked for a week, so that my departure from HRA would not be precipitous and said so long to my staff and Hank Foley.

Chapter Ten

A New Epidemic

1979-1981

It was a brand new experience being the public information officer for an administrative office rather than for a program, but it wasn't too difficult, because I knew most of the twelve people of my new staff. It wasn't long before I did notice something that bothered me. There was a flow of news releases that came through the office of which most were of no great significance. There were countless releases that simply were announcing appointments to minor offices. Each of them had to be reviewed, logged in and forwarded to the Department public information office for approval. It seemed as a colossal waste of effort, paper and time.

With the departure of Califano, a new crew had descended on the Department. Pat Harris was Secretary and her Assistant Secretary for Public Information was a fellow named Bill Wise. After a few weeks, I asked Bill Wise if we could cut off this avalanche of paper. At first, he wasn't sure he wanted to give me the authority, but finally he agreed as long as I kept a log of the releases with only those personnel announcements for Bureau heads going forward. With his agreement, I called my first staff meeting of the PHS information officers to inform them of the change at which I emphasized that the authority was being extended only as long as there was good behavior. If anyone abused the authority, we would go back to the old system.

It was a small step, but it reduced the flow of paper greatly.

There was one flow of paper that did not stop. Various organizations coming up with special occasions wrote to the White House asking for a letter recognizing the event. Those letters, usually from hospitals, landing in our office to draft a reply for the President. The first time I became aware of this was when, Bob Proctor, of the staff was complaining about "another one of these!" After he explained what was needed, I pointed out that these were the people who were paying our salaries. I took his draft of the reply and decided to call the hospital which would be celebrating its 50th year in operation and ask of what during the 50 years they were most proud of. I was a little surprised after I indentified why I was calling to hear the impressed reply from the hospital administrator. From then on, I asked the staff to personalize the letter when drafting what used to be a pro forma reply.

Since I was the Public Information Officer for the Public Health Service, I had to undergo a security check so that in the event I came across anything marked "Confidential" or "Secret" I could legitimately read it. I told Dr. Richmond that the whole exercise seemed like overkill, but to prove I was wrong, he shared with me a fascinating memorandum he had written after a one hour and ten minute meeting with Fidel Castro marked "Confidential." Before reading the memo, I said, "He spoke a lot, didn't he."

"No" Dr. Richmond said, "He listened and asked very informed questions."

The copy of the memorandum he shared with me concluded, ..."one gets the feeling of a very well informed, energetic and dynamic, dedicated person. In contrast to the image purveyed in the media of a loud, verbose person, he was quiet in demeanor and speech and a very good listener."

It was at Dr. Richmond's staff meeting that I learned of the beginning of a new epidemic, although, neither I nor anyone else realized it at that time. Bill Foege, the Director of the Centers for Disease Control (CDC) said that there was a report of three cases of Kaposi's Sarcoma in New York, and he was sending a team to investigate. As the meeting was breaking up, I asked him what Kaposi's Sarcoma was, and he carefully explained to me that it was a form of cancer.

"But why would three cases cause any worry?" I asked showing my ignorance.

Once again, he patiently explained that the disease which usually affected older men was showing up in young, white men which should not be happening and three cases all at once was out of the ordinary. Something was very wrong. At the time, I don't think any more of it, but later I realized what we were seeing was the beginning of the AIDs epidemic that was to grip this country and the efforts of the public health community for years to come.

As the summer got underway, the nation began to experience an intense heat wave which eventually posed a great health threat especially to older people. I suggested to Dr. Richmond that it might be a good idea to issue a news release giving advice to the public about how to prevent the serious effects of dehydration. He agreed and, with advice from the experts at NIH, we issued the warning.

Sydney Wolfe, from the organization Public Citizen, who never missed any opportunity to challenge a government action, promptly issued a challenge to the release. He took issue with the statement that the elderly should "use common sense" in dealing with the heat. He argued, correctly as it turned out, that people, especially the elderly, should drink more liquids that they ever would consider normal. When I checked with the people at NIH, they said that Wolfe was correct. In fact, when he worked there, he did work on how heat affected people. It became part of my learning experience.

A short time later, the investigators at CDC began to see an outbreak of cases of toxic shock syndrome (TSS). Altogether, there were about 890 reported cases of women succumbing with the death of 35. Doctors at CDC suspected a connection between TSS and the use of tampons. After careful analysis, they confirmed this connection especially those produced by Proctor and Gamble under the trademark name of Rely. Of course, P & G denied the connection and at first resisted any public announcement. The PHS was ready to make this public when, unknown to us, the FDA group at CDC, probably yielding to jurisdictional jealousies, cast doubt on the findings. Wayne Pines, an excellent public information officer, had gone to Bill Wise relaying FDA suspicions bypassing our office. This called a halt to any public announcement.

Dr. Richmond called a hasty meeting between CDC and FDA. Wayne and I were included at the meeting where the FDA Commissioner, Jere Goyan, who had reviewed the results of the study, agreed with the findings and agreed a public announcement was necessary. I motioned to Wayne to come with me. When we were in my office with the door closed, I told Wayne that his communication with the Office of the Secretary on a matter of public health without going through the surgeon general's office was out of line, and that in the future, "all communications between FDA and the Department had to go through my office."

When Wayne objected saying that there often was no time to waste of some matters, my one word answer to him was, "Bullshit." Then I added, "If you want me to, I'll put it in writing." I then told him that Dr. Richmond wanted to have him fired until I persuaded him not to. Then, with Wayne sitting there, I phoned Bill Wise and told him that all communications between Wayne's office and him on public health matters would have to go through my office so that we didn't get caught once again between organizational competitions.

The next day, the public announcement, with P & Gs still objecting, was made. In fact, P & G even commissioned a study to prove that the Rely Tampons were safe for women to use. That study, when reviewed by scientists, was found to be as flawed as were the Rely Tampons.

The normal routine of our office was suddenly interrupted when I received a worried Saturday morning phone call from Storm Whaley, the Public Information Officer for the National Institutes of Health. During a sleep experiment, a young woman participant had died. Word had gotten out, and the press was clamoring for access to her medical records. I phoned Dr, Richmond to advise him before going out to NIH, and he gave me the valuable advice that we were to "protect the privacy of the dead woman's parents."

The distraught parents were willing to have NIH release the young woman's medical records but not her psychiatric files. But that wasn't what was bothering Storm Whaley at the moment. It was reporter Chris Russell's demand that she be given priority in gaining the records because she had asked for them first.

I agreed with Whaley that we couldn't give precedence to any one reporter, but if we released the medical records at 11:00 AM, Chris Russell who worked for the *Evening Star* would get her lead. When I called her to tell her we had to release all records to everyone at the same time, she began shouting that she had asked for them first. I interrupted her and told her to calm down. Then informed her the release would be at 11:00 AM which made her happy.

But that wasn't the end of it, for when we released the medical but not the psychiatric records, I received a demanding call from the *Star's* attorney demanding all records saying, "you don't mean to tell me that a dead person has any right to privacy?"

"No" I replied remembering Dr. Richmond's order, "but the living parents do." That ended the conversation with the attorney threatening to see us in court. When I reported the conversation to the General Counsel's office, the lawyer there said, that was a standard threat, and no more was heard about it.

Then Ted Cron struck again. He was the information officer at the Federal Trade Commission with Mike Pertschuck the Commissioner. As he had done so many times before, he found that the Commissioner wasn't carrying out his duties as Ted thought he should. He spoke up and was moved from his position to one where he could do no harm. Knowing that Ted was an excellent writer, I signed him up to be the Surgeon General's speechwriter. With the change in Administration after the 1980 elections, it eventually turned out to be a very good move.

Before the election, during a meeting with Secretary Harris, where we were reviewing some data about maternal and child health, she wondered why we always had such negative information to pass out to the public. "Wouldn't it be good if we could give them some positive information?" she mused. It was that softly expressed hope that led to one of our efforts growing from a small idea into a national movement.

Taking her expressed wish, I outlined a plan to gather a number of organizations together with an interest in maternal and child health in an effort to share information and efforts to improve their health suggesting we call it "The Healthy Babies Coalition." When one feminist, Jules Janice, in the Surgeon General's office heard this, she made the sensible suggestion to add "mothers" to the title, and we were ready to launch "The Healthy Mothers, Healthy Babies Coalition."

As we were considering that project, I approached Dr. Richmond with another suggestion. I asked him if he was interested in starting a new institution. There had been a number of White House Conferences--Children and Youth, Aging, Medical Costs. But what if we had a Surgeon

General's Workshop where we gathered together a group of experts in a field to examine a public health project and issue a report that would then become part of the literature and could be used as a platform for action. He liked the idea and asked me to give him a proposal in writing.

As I was finishing the proposal, Woodie Kessel, a pediatrician who was on the staff approached me. He had heard what I had proposed and asked if he could add his name to the memo. I thought it was an odd request but couldn't care less and said it was OK. I learned years later that he was claiming credit for originating the idea. Oh well!

Dr. Richmond liked the idea and gave us the go ahead. Dr. Vince Hutchins, the head of the Bureau of Maternal and Child Health was the logical and brilliant choice to head up the effort, and it was there that I found in him one of the ideal public servants who put the effort to improve the programs that served women and children ahead of any bureaucratic hurdles. In working together on this project, I found a very dear friend.

As we put the staff together to run the workshop, I knew we needed someone who could handle the numerous details of organizing the project, so I asked Dr. Richmond's office to request that Florence Foelak be detailed to us to handle all the myriad details of the workshop. It proved to be one of our better selections, since she turned out to be a whiz. The rest of the small staff consisted of Carol Galaty and Woodie Kessel. Vince Hutchins was busy between keeping one eye on the Bureau he ran and putting together a planning committee for the workshop. It was as we were putting the details in place that our national elections took place, and Ronald Reagan defeated Jimmie Carter for president. Since the workshop was scheduled to take place in mid-December, I knew that we had to get the report of the conference out very quickly.

In rounding up the funds to run the workshop, we asked the appropriate PHS agencies to contribute. All except NIH's National Institute of Child Health and Human Development (NICHD) were eager to help. It was then that I learned the value of polite blackmail. As we put together the advisory committee, we neglected to have any representative from that Institute on the committee. They protested, they contributed and they were included.

With the workshop underway at the hotel in Reston, I met two physicians with whom I would cross paths in the years ahead. One was Dr. George Ryan, president of the American College of Obstetricians and Gynecologists (ACOG). The other was Dr. Ezra Davidson who led the steering committee for the Workshop and who would be a future president of ACOG.

On the final day of the workshop, I told the attendees that we would get each one a copy of the report as soon as it came off the press. It was then that Dr. Ryan made a request that was taken up unanimously. He wanted enough copies to distribute to all officials of ACOG. With all others wanting equal treatment, I asked them to write me with their requirements, and we would try to fill all their requests. So with a silent prayer, I hoped we could fulfill their requests.

I negotiated with the Department's Printing Officer to have the report printed and distributed within 30 days of the time we delivered the proofs to him telling him that Dr. Richmond wanted it out that quickly. To meet that deadline, I hired Fritz Witte, a former newspaper man who had worked for the FDA, to gather all the papers as they were delivered and write accounts of them overnight so the presenters could read and approve them.

With Fritz Witte doing his job efficiently and Florence gathering the reports from the panels, we were ready to tackle putting the report together in the record time that the change of administration demanded. Fritz ran into one problem with the representative from CDC dragging his heels on giving approval to Fritz's summary of his presentation. Once again, I resorted to polite blackmail telling the recalcitrant that we would have to leave his presentation out of the final report. His approval came forthwith.

Then it was a race to put the report in form for printing. I took this time to come down with a cold, so by phone and face to face consultation with Dr. Hutchins over my sickbed, we were able to get the manuscript to the printer on time. With the proofs then in our hands, Florence, Vince and I did some very fast proofreading. And it was 30 days later when, Florence, holding copies of the printed report in the air, exulted, "We did it!"

With the change in Administration a whole new group of actors came onto the Washington stage. Whereas Dr. Richmond had held down the combined jobs of Assistant Secretary of Health and Surgeon General, the new setup split the jobs with Dr. Ed Brandt becoming the Assistant Secretary of health and Dr. Everett Koop, a brilliant pediatric surgeon and a supporter of the anti-abortion movement nominated for Surgeon General as a political payoff to the Right to Life movement that had supported Reagan.

When I met with Dr. Brandt for the first time, he told me that Bob Hardesty who was working at the LBJ Presidential Library had told him he was getting a good public information man. It surprised me since I barely knew Hardesty, but I did know and had worked with his brother Jack.

At one of our early meetings, I raised the question of how we were going to handle the many speech requests that were coming in. He said, "Why don't we give precedence to those who'll pay my way?" I must have shaken my head "no", because he wanted to know why I didn't think it was a good idea since it would help with the budget. I then explained, "Ed, they're not asking you because they like the way you part your hair. They will want to do business with you, and I don't think you should put yourself in that position."

He listened to me and agreed. And that agreement was going to play out a year later when he had to call the FDA Commissioner, Dr. Arthur Hayes Jr. on the carpet for accepting paid trips to make speeches and also claiming official expenses for the trip. When he told me about it, he said he was thinking of my advice when he had to chastise Hayes.

Shortly after Dr. Koop was nominated, he handed me a speech he had given of which he was obviously proud. Reading it, I was stunned at his dystopian view of the role government was playing with women's reproductive rights. I made the mistake of showing it to Ted Cron and another member of my staff, Elaine Arkin. A few weeks later, an obviously angry Dr. Koop accosted me and accused me of spreading that speech around to damage his chances of being confirmed. I was startled and pled my innocence, but I told him I had shared it with a few people and I would check. After checking with Ted and Elaine, I was pretty sure that Elaine may have been the one. I went to Koop and apologized, but, as Ted told me much later, "Koop never forgives and he never forgets." Ted went on to become a valued confident to Dr. Koop advising him to become the Surgeon General for all the people and not just for his friends in the anti-abortion movement.

Another newcomer was Mrs. Marjorie Mecklenberg, another member of the anti-abortion group that was filling the ranks. She had been nominated to head the Office of Population Affairs. The word came down that she was to give no interviews before she was confirmed. Much to no one's surprise, I received a call from a reporter from the *Evening Star* asking for an interview. I told her that I was going to tell the reporter that she would be giving no interviews at this time. She asks me if she could talk to him and explain why. In my innocence, I agreed.

The next day, there appeared in the *Star* a full blown interview. After the day's staff meeting, I asked her to join me in my office and demanded to know why she had given the interview. She blathered a bit and never gave anything resembling an answer. Later that day, I received a dressing down by the newly installed deputy public affairs officer for the Department. Mrs. Mecklenberg went on to become a discredited leader of that office using official travel for her personal affairs like going to her son's football games in Colorado.

My good friend, Charlie Miller, had served many administrations both Republican and Democratic with distinction. He was a bureaucrat with complete integrity, so when the first Reagan budget was unveiled with drastic cuts in public health programs, he felt that he could not in good faith defend those cuts before congressional committees, so he promptly submitted his resignation much to Dr. Brandt's dismay. And, although I was extremely sorry to see him leave, I could only admire his devotion to his ethical sense of what was right.

During the last days of the Carter Administration, Bob Hutchings who was working in the Office on Smoking and Health, was working with the Clinton E. Frank advertising company in Chicago to develop a campaign to encourage young girls to stop or avoid smoking. The campaign was designed around the beautiful movie star and model, Brooke Shields, who gave her services for the nominal fee of $1 for the poster and $500 for the television ads. The project had been accepted by Dr.

Richmond and Secretary Pat Harris, but I spoke to Bob and thought it would be good to get approval from the new crew.

Dr. Brandt reviewed the material, a poster of Miss Shields in a white jump suit with cigarettes in her ears and the headline, "Smoking Spoils Your Looks" and two televisions spots, 30 seconds and 10 seconds. The 10 second one showing her drying her washed hair saying, "If there's anything I hate it's washing my hair and then being with people who smoke...Yuck!" He not only approved them but thought they would be effective.

So from there, the campaign was sent up to the secretary's office where it languished. After waiting for several weeks without receiving any response, I had a meeting with the woman who was the Assistant Secretary for Public Affairs and asked her if she had any problem with the ads. I really wasn't prepared for her answer. Yes, she had a problem. Brooke Shields had played the part of a teen age prostitute in the motion picture "Pretty Baby."

"How do you think the Moral Majority who supported us at the Republican Convention would feel if we approved this?"

Astonished, I tried to argue that she was an actress playing a role. In real life, she was a cheerleader at her high school. But my argument was falling on deaf ears. I asked them not to make a final decision until Dr. Brandt returned from Geneva where he was attending a World Health Organization meeting, but I really knew that the decision had already been made.

As soon as I returned to my office, I wrote a memo to her pointing out what the public response would be if the Department turned down this effort. After that. I phoned Bob Hutchings to let him know what was happening and suggested, although he was way ahead of me, that they get in touch with the American Lung Association to see if they would pick up the campaign. That's what he did, and that's what they did, but not before the officials at DHHS had issued a statement that the campaign was ineffective. In a letter to Richard Sinsheimer, the president of the American Lung Association, David Newhall III, Chief of Staff for the Department, offered to grant them the right to use the campaign but commented, "A decision was made to cancel the two Brooke Shields efforts because we did not think the spots would do an effective job of curbing teenage smoking..."

Comments like these from DHHS really hurt the creative staff at the advertising agency. They knew the campaign was brilliant, and their testing showed that it would be effective. When I heard this, I told Bob I would like to go to Chicago and meet with the staff to explain what had happened. We did that and when I addressed the staff, I started by saying that the poster and 10 second spot were the most creative and effective we had ever seen and that the comments from the Department did not reflect reality. I then explained what had happened and why. I also pointed out that the controversy, when it hit the news, gave more visibility to the campaign as controversy usually does.

It was after this that I told Eileen that if nothing else developed before the end of the year, I was going to leave the government, I had had it with these people. I prepared my resume and dug into my job running the public information office at PHS.

Shortly after this nonsense, Vince Hutchins called to say that an organizational meeting for the Healthy Mothers, Healthy Babies Coalition was scheduled at the March of Dimes headquarters at White Plains, NY. Attending the meeting, in addition to the two of us and the March of Dimes, would be representatives from The Academy of Pediatrics, the Salvation Army and the American College of Obstetricians and Gynecologists(ACOG).

At the meeting, after a general discussion of the health needs of women and children, they turned to me to tell them how we thought the organization should be formed. I said the coalition should be open to any national organization that had an interest in maternal and child health and which had a network of regional or statewide affiliates. I also emphasized that these organizations should be committed to sharing information about their activities with all members. It was from this meeting that the coalition was formed that eventually embraced about 20 national organizations with statewide coalitions in almost every state.

Vince Hutchins knew that I was ready to leave government service and that ACOG was in the process of moving its headquarters from Chicago to Washington. He spoke to Warren Pearse, ACOG's Executive Director, and asked him if they were looking for a public information officer. Warren told him they had one, but he thought she may not want to move. It was then that Vince introduced me to Warren who asked me to send him my resume. I dug in my briefcase and handed one to him. It was about three weeks later when he came to my office to see if I were still interested. He had to check with ACOG's president, George Ryan, whom I had met at the Surgeon General's Workshop.

A short time later, I was offered the position which I accepted. I immediately informed Dr. Brandt that I would be leaving, and he tried to get me to change my mind. but I said to him, "Ed, I'm doing you a favor, because they will be telling you to get rid of me soon." I would be leaving, but Dr. Brandt and I would continue to meet for lunch from time to time to settle the world's affairs.

Representative John Dingell, the Michigan Democrat had scheduled hearings into the Brooke Shield debacle. As part of his investigation, he sent two House investigators to DHHS, and I was called to give information. When I arrived in the conference room, I was greeted by a representative from DHHS General Counsel's office and was informed that he was there to see that I would not incriminate myself with one of my answers. I declined his assistance saying that I did not need any one since my answers would be completely truthful. He went into the other room to call his office and returned saying his services weren't really needed. I was on my own.

The investigators were pushing to find the Tobacco Institute's hand in the cancelling of the Shields' campaign, and I kept telling them that no one from the Tobacco Institute needed to intervene, because the tobacco people had all the help they needed here in DHHS. I told them of my conversation that revealed the fear of the Moral Majority's reaction, but they weren't really interested in that: they wanted to find a tobacco connection.

It was then that I mentioned my memo which warned the DHHS officials of what would happen in the campaign was cancelled. They wanted to know "What memo?" I pointed to the file they had and told them it was in there. They shook their heads and handed me the file. I flipped through it only to find that the numbskulls had doctored the file and left my memo out. I told the investigators that the file had been doctored and called my office to asked my secretary to make a copy of the memo and bring it down. After I handed the memo to them, and after a few more questions, my part in the investigation was over.

I returned to our offices and went to Dr. Brandt's. he took one look at me and asked what was wrong. I told him that the file had been doctored."Ed" I said, "I'm glad I don't have to work with these people anymore. I'm just sorry you do." A few days later, about 30 years after I took the government job until I could find a real one, I left government service.

Chapter Eleven
That Rollicking Fun Timing Group 1981-1991

When I knew I was going to leave the government and become the Director of Public information for the American College of Obstetrics and Gynecology (ACOG), I knew that I wanted to convince Florence Foelak to join me. She had been such a fine person to handle the details at the Surgeon General's Workshop that I realized she would be invaluable doing the same thing with me at ACOG. There also was a window of opportunity to retire for government workers that was going to expire shortly, so I urged her to take the opportunity and come to ACOG with me. She finally agreed, and we began building a small staff which, in addition to the two of us, would consist of a press officer and a secretary.

On our first day together in our new positions, I cautioned her by acknowledging that I wasn't sure I knew what we would be doing and said, "I hope we won't be bored here." It wasn't too long before we put that caution behind us. Laurie Hall was to be our press officer.

Although I had left the government, affairs there followed me to my new position. The people who I thankfully left behind in DHHS decided to remove Wayne Pines from FDA and reassign him to the National Institute of Mental Health with the specious excuse that "his skills could be used effectively in NIMH." The editor of the newsletter *Food Chemical News* called me for my comments, and I was quoted accurately as saying, "Anyone who believes the official PHS statement will probably willing to believe that the Brooklyn Bridge is for sale for one dollar" and went on to defend Wayne's excellent professionalism.

With that distraction behind me, I thought it might be a good idea to write a weekly column under ACOG's president's by-line which we called "Women's Health" and offer it at no cost to the nation's daily newspapers. The initial offering was a letter offering this service and included the first four columns that were dated for release one week at a time. Florence took care of finding a printer who would print the columns in two formats: one that could be printed directly from photo ready copy; the other being a typed script which the newspaper could set in its own type. She also located a mailing list of the country's daily newspapers which we could rent.

With this in place, I described what I wanted to do to Warren Pearse and got his OK to give me the budget. I also approached one of the College's medical directors, Keith White, who agreed to review the columns for accuracy. The only other review would be by the ACOG president. With this all in place, we sent out the first mailing to the country's 1500 daily newspapers. Within a very short time, the acceptances came rolling in, and we had more than 300 papers which wanted to try the columns. We were on our way. Eventually, we expanded our mailing lists to make the offer to weekly papers. By the time we were finished, the "Women's Health" column was appearing every week in about 1,000 papers in North and Central America.

Every year ACOG held an annual clinical meeting (ACM) at which scholarly and technical presentations were made. As we prepared for our first time to organize the press room for the event, we ran into something for which we were unprepared. Florence went to the people who were running the ACM and asked for copies of the papers that were going to be presented and ran into a blank wall. It seems there was a reluctance to share these papers with the press.

I had a meeting with the doctor who was the lead for the scientific sessions who explained that press reports might in effect ruin the investigator's chances of having his or her paper published in a scholarly journal. I pointed out that the so-called Inglefinger Rule, named after the editor of the *New England Journal of Medicine*, said that news reports of presentations at medical meetings would not interfere with future publication. With some reluctance, they gave us permission to have the papers which we could copy for distribution to the press.

But what this revealed, and it was something with which we were going to have to deal, was the feeling by many members of the profession that the press was, in a way, their enemy and not to be trusted.

We went ahead and planned for our first expedition to Dallas to establish our press room. Florence carefully laid out all the copies of the scientific papers she had prepared, but before we opened to the press, Dr. Mary Jo Sullivan who, obviously had been tipped off that we were going to give copies of the presentations to the press, visited us to inspect the papers with obvious suspicion. Once again, I explained the Inglefinger Rule and pointed out that we had removed any diagrams and charts but letting the reporters have copies of the papers would only help insure accuracy in their reporting. In addition to making the papers available, we picked out those that had the most news value and asked the authors to give brief news conferences. That was the procedure we were able to follow for the next ten years.

We were to run into two stumbles at the ACM in the years ahead. The first took place in the annual meeting in San Francisco. Although the exhibit floor was billed as an educational display, one pharmaceutical company, to attract more doctors to its exhibit, had an enclosed golf driving range with a golf pro who would educate the doctors on how to drive their golf balls far and with accuracy. Since a press badge was all the press needed for access to the exhibit hall, the next day, the CBS TV station had a delightful expose of ACOG's doctors being instructed on the ins and outs of driving a golf ball.

The medical director who was responsible for the exhibit hall accosted me saying, "Lebow, you loused up!" When I asked him why, he told me I should not have allowed the TV crew into the exhibit hall. My answer with real fervor was, "No. You loused up by allowing that drug company to put up that exhibit!"

The other, and much more important event was a paper given by one of our doctors promoting a particular drug. The doctor failed to mention, as good practice would dictate, that he had been paid to do the paper by that same drug company. In addition, the company's representative had obtained press credentials and issued a news release stating that ACOG had endorsed the use of that item. It was a question of locking the barn door after the horse was stolen, but we notified the company that they could no longer get press credentials, and our in house lawyer, Ann Allen, wrote to the company's president effectively telling them to cease and desist.

One other experience, but a pleasant one, occurred when the former President Gerald Ford agreed to give an address to the ACM. My son, Edward, asked me to get his autograph. When I asked him "Why?", he pointed out that he was the only non-elected president we have ever had. So, with a photograph I had obtained, I asked President Ford if he would autograph the photo for my son which is what he did inscribing the photo "To Ed."

Some time later, to try to help the doctors get over their aversion to dealing with the press, I was able to contract with someone who would give the assembled doctors a taste of how to submit to interviews successfully. After the session was over, Keith White wanted to know why I couldn't do the same for ACOG's members. That, eventually, opened up a completely new effort with Florence running the camera on the recipients of my grilling in between discussions of interview strategy.

The year I joined ACOG, it was due to host the international meeting of ob/gyns in San Francisco. The officious woman who Warren put in charge of organizing the meeting wanted me run the press room by myself. I met with her and Warren and suggested that I could locate a public relations outfit in San Francisco to run it on contract, but it would be chaotic for me to try to run it by myself with no backup. Warren wisely said I could bring Florence, and, as it turned out, it was a fortunate decision.

Warren also asked me if I could see if Ed Brandt would be willing to give the keynote address to the meeting. I called him, and when he accepted, I told him that we would pay his way. With both of us laughing, he said that I knew better than that. I told him I was just testing to see if he still was taking my advice.

As we ran the news room at the conference, two events showed how valuable the decision to include Florence was. She was confronted one morning by two very frightened doctors from Taiwan. The official program, in error, identified them as representing Mainland China. Florence assured them we would rectify the error, although at the time, she didn't know how we were going to do it. When she told me what had happened, I sought out the woman who arranged the conference and found she wanted to have nothing to do with changing the identification in the program.

Florence then whited out the words that identified them coming from the mainland and substituted their correct identification. We then drafted a news release admitting to our error which we could hand to them without ever releasing it as well as a letter addressed to each of them apologizing and taking the blame for the mistake. After Florence gave them the corrected programs with our news release and letters of apology, Florence said, "I thank God that we live in this country."

It was shortly after that an indignant doctor from Mainland China put in his appearance demanding satisfaction that we were glad to give him the revised package of material that we had in hand.

Then Ed Brandt gave his keynote address. It was the next day that I received an indignant phone call from my successor at DHHS wanting to know why I had allowed the story that made headlines in the San Francisco newspapers in which Dr. Keith Russell, the California sponsor of the meeting, criticized Dr. Brandt and the Reagan Administration for their health policies. I told her I would check it out and found that, indeed, Russell had spoken out of turn. I sought him out and explained that we had a severe public relations problem on our hands, and my relations with Dr. Brandt would be damaged if there was no immediate apology. He was abashed and agreed to sign a letter to Dr. Brandt which I dictated to Florence in which he not only apologized to Dr. Brandt for "an off the cuff comment that he should not have made in answer to a reporter's question" but had also apologized to me as well.

Back in Washington, ACOG had a new president, Dr. James Breen. I had been successful in convincing the incoming presidents that they should pick a theme for their one year as president and stick to it rather than wander all around without any singular focus during their term of office. He had selected the theme of the Aging Population of Women and its meaning for the future of ob.gyn. Although Jim believed that abortion was wrong, when the College submitted an amicus brief to the Supreme Court supporting Planned Parenthood in their challenge to Pennsylvania's Abortion Control Act, he, as a good soldier representing the College, agreed to hold a news conference outlining the College's position.

Toward the end of the news conference, Linda Greenhouse, *NY Times* excellent reporter who covered the Supreme Court, came rushing in. Since she had missed most of the conference, she asked if she could sit down with Dr. Breen for an interview. I explained that we had to rush over to a TV station for another interview but she would be welcome to join us in the cab. Which is what she did. As she questioned him, he said, "Look, if my 16 year old daughter became pregnant, she would have an abortion tomorrow." Linda, who could have used that quote without violating any journalistic standard, turned to me and asked, "Can I use that?" Since he hadn't said it was "off the record," I gave her the go ahead. Unfortunately for him, when it appeared in her story the next day, he was in hot water with his Right to Life friends, but I always admired her, not only for her excellent reporting but for her honesty in even bothering to ask permission.

Since the College had submitted its brief in the case, we were permitted to attend the oral arguments in the case, and I was fortunate enough to snag one of the seats where I had the unforgettable experience of watching the nine justices rush to their seats and conduct the grilling of the lawyers on both sides. It was several months later when the Court decided in a 5 to 4 decisions that, although states could place some reasonable restrictions on the practice of abortion, in a decision jointly written by Justices Sandra Day O'Conner, Anthony M. Kennedy and David H. Souter, they stated that "the essential holding of Roe v. Wade should be retained and once again reaffirmed."

It was with the election of ACOG's next president that the college moved firmly into the twentieth century. For the first time, ACOG would have a woman president. Dr. Luella (Teddy) Klein was chief of Ob/Gyn at Grady Hospital in Atlanta, Georgia. When I met with her to discuss how we were going to handle her presidency, she asked what I thought her theme for the year should be.

"Anything but women in ob/gyn." I answered.

"But that's what my friends want me to talk about."

I explained that when she got up nobody would mistake her for a man. And if she talked about women in ob/gyn, she would essentially be saying, 'I got here because I'm a woman and not because I'm a successful professional.'"

From that conversation, ACOG moved from its position as a trade organization interested in protecting its own interests to a profession concerned with the welfare of America's women, because she choose as her theme, unintended pregnancy. Her presidential address which she drafted pointed out that 55% of all pregnancies in the US during the preceding year were unintended and in many cases unwanted, and she called on ACOG and the country to attack this problem.

Because of the combination of Dr. Klein as the first female president of ACOG and her selection of unintended pregnancy as her theme for the year, she receive much attention in the media. As things spooled out, I suggested that we develop a public information program around unintended pregnancy. She was willing, and I began fleshing out a proposal to submit to our executive board. We were going to ask for $100,000 to mount the campaign in the first year.

At the board meeting, she handed the presentation over to me. I explained what we wanted to do, and specified three conditions. First, the money should come from ACOG and not from any pharmaceutical company so that no one could say we were shilling for a drug company; second, if the program succeeded, we should be able to say we were not doing this to increase our members business but because it would be good for the health of the nation's women and families; and third, it not be a one year but a three year program. Surprisingly, with almost no discussion, the board gave us their go ahead. And we were off and running.

The first thing we did was to contract with the Gallup organization in Princeton to conduct a nationwide telephone survey to find out what the public knew and their attitudes about contraception. As we worked out the questions with the Gallup expert, we emerged with nine questions. He said, "You still have one question you can use," so we carefully constructed the final question.

"At what grade, if at all, should sex education be taught in school?" The choices ran from: "Not at all" to "Primary School, Junior High School, Senior High School and College."

I asked the Gallup people to compare our results with the results of previous polls, but they informed me that ours was the first to ask these questions. Then the results came in from a nationally representative sample of about 1,000 women and 500 men. By a better than three to one margin, American women believed there were "substantial risks" involved with using the birth control pill with three fourths of women under age 35 believing this, and three quarters of college educated women felt the same in spite of the statistical evidence to the contrary. Cancer, blood clots, weight gain and high blood pressure were the stated risks. Nearly half of women felt that the risks from the pill were greater than the risks of childbearing. In spite of these findings, three fourths of men and women agreed that sexually active teenagers should have access to contraceptive services.

When it came to that added question about at what grade should sex education be taught, we hit the jackpot with roughly half feeling it should begin in elementary school, and another quarter believing junior high was an appropriate time to begin such instruction. Fewer than one in ten believed it should not be taught at all. With that, we felt we had identified the Moral Majority.

Before we held a news conference to announce the result of the survey, we contracted with a Chicago company that specialized in such things to produce a slide chart to show the "Benefits, Risks & Effectiveness of Contraception." We offered it to all ACOG doctors and made it part of the press package. Needless to say, this gadget became very popular.

With this under our belts, we turned to the job of producing a national public information program to combat unintended pregnancies that Dr. Klein had called for. I got in touch with Paul Brickman whom I had met during the Brooke Shields fiasco and was now with Martin Janis, a Chicago ad agency. Working with them, we produced a television public service announcement, radio spots, newspaper ads and a leaflet entitled "The Facts: What You Need to Know About Contraceptives to Make the Right Choice."

The TV spot, which was to anchor the effort and was to be the cause of the great controversy, opened with a young girl getting on a school bus saying "I intend to become president." The next young woman in an office saying "I intend to go back to school." The third with another, very pregnant young woman setting a dinner table saying "I intended to have a family...but not this soon." Then an announcer said "Nothing changes intentions faster than an unintended pregnancy. Unintended pregnancies are riskier than any of today's contraceptives." This was followed by a pitch to call the 800 number 1-800-Intends" for a copy of the pamphlet "The Facts."

Dr Klein asked me if the networks would accept the spots, and I told her that they had an unwritten policy against airing any spots relating to contraceptives, but I hoped perhaps this would be a breakthrough. Knowing the odds against us, we prepared an information packet that we sent to all ACOG District officers and to every one of the 50 State Health Officers asking for their cooperation in this effort to combat unintended pregnancies. Then, Paul Brickman and I visited the three major TV networks. And, one after the other, they turned us down.

The next step was to hold a news conference in New York announcing our attack on the problem of unintended pregnancies and, by the way, that all TV networks had turned their backs on this effort. The news conference was well attended: the AP, UPI, *New York Times, Los Angeles Times,* ABC and CBS radio news, National Public Radio and several women's magazines as well as the advertising press were in attendance. After Dr. Klein gave a brief statement and said she had written to the presidents of the networks asking them to reconsider their refusal to air the spot, we showed the TV spot; the first question from a bewildered reporter was, "What's wrong with the spot?" And we said they would have to ask the networks, because we thought it should be non-controversial.

After the conference, Dr. Klein, Paul Brickman and I went to lunch at the Tavern on the Green. While we were waiting for our lunch to be served, I thought I should check with the office. When I called, Florence said, "What did you do in New York!!!" She then told me that for the past 30 minutes all the phone lines lit up with everyone demanding to see the now controversial TV ad. The wire services had spread the word, and one of the requests came from ABC News which serviced the 200 or so ABC affiliated stations around the country. She gave me the address and the person's name so that I could deliver the tape that afternoon.

Then for the next several weeks, an avalanche of editorials, op-ed pieces and letters to the editor rocked the country. The *NY Times* ran a news story and an editorial. The *Boston Globe* had a cartoon and an editorial. The *Atlanta Journal and Constitution* chimed in. The conservative George Wills wrote as did the liberal Ellen Goodman. In all we collected about 250 clippings that amazed us with the unanimity of all condemning the networks. In a country as diverse as ours, there was not a single one taking the side of the networks. Perhaps my favorite one was from the *Dayton Daily News* which wrote, "The ads were created not be the producers of soap operas, mind you, but by that rollicking group of fun-timers known as the American College of Obstetricians and Gynecologists."

There were three major themes reflected in these articles: the first was the constant advertisement of the 800 number; then the acknowledgement that ACOG was spending its own money; and finally, that ACOG was not doing this to drum up more business but to perform a public service. We couldn't have asked for better.

By the end of the year, with Florence handling all negotiations with the Chicago firm handling the requests for "The Facts" pamphlet, we had received more than 35,000 calls.

It was shortly after the negative press deluge that Dr. Klein received a call from the NBC official who seemed to be saying that NBC hadn't turned down the spot. She referred him to me. When he once again tried to say that NBC hadn't turned us down, I gave him the date of our visit, he then said that the next time we were in NY, why didn't we drop in to get it straightened out. Since Washington and NY aren't that far apart, we scheduled a meeting.

Dr. Klein, Paul Brickman and I met before going to the NBC offices not expecting much from the meeting. Unknown to us, and something I found years later, the CEO of NBC had directed the people with whom we were to meet "to find some way of working with these people." As we introduced ourselves, I led off the discussion by saying, "We are not saying that everything that's wrong with the world is the fault of TV, we are just saying we disagree on this issue."

Then, we were pleasantly surprised when we were asked, "Would you be willing to revise your announcement?" I said we would if the integrity of the spot wasn't negated. And that's what we did. On leaving NBC, Dr. Klein said with obvious pleasure, "We actually got them to change their policy."

After some negotiation, we agreed to substitute the announcer's statement "Unintended pregnancy is more dangerous than any of today's contraceptives" with "There are many ways to prevent an unintended pregnancy." With that agreement, NBC also volunteered their Chicago studios in making the change. We were then ready for the next step in convincing the NBC officials to take part in a news conference announcing our agreement. CBS, upon hearing of the intended news conference, asked to see the revised spot and quickly gave approval. ABC came along later. Not only did the three major networks agree to cooperate, but they actually gave the spot good coverage with CBS even placing it during an NFL Sunday game.

The result pleased everyone except Florence who never was one to tell me when she thought I had done something wrong when she accused me of "selling out to the networks." It was a statement we would laugh about for years to come.

As the furor with the networks abated, the South Carolina District of ACOG came up with an idea to use the Reverend Jesse Jackson as a spokesman to help reduce unintended pregnancies among minority young people. The District chairman had been at a meeting where he had spoken and approached him with the idea. He seemed to be receptive to doing a TV spot for us and told our man to arrange it with his assistant. And that's where things began going wrong.

When Rev Jackson's assistant was approached, he informed the ACOG people that Rev Jackson's time was valuable, so it would be necessary to reimburse him for his time. The $1,000 offer was refused out of hand. Eventually, the offered price was $5,000. At that point, feeling they were being fleeced, I advised them to forget about it, but they had the bit in their teeth and eventually agreed to pay $10,000 if he would do two spots for us: one aimed at young men, the other at young women.

With that agreement, I had to put together a production team, and Florence with her contacts arranged that. I wrote to Jackson with two proposed scripts, but suggested that with his experience, he might want to put the production in his own words. We set a date and a place and were ready to go. When the Rev. Jackson and his entourage appeared at the studio, it became obvious that he hadn't read the prepared scripts when he said, "Where are the boards?" So I dutifully created two boards from which he could read.

As we were ready to go, he clapped his hands and said, "Let's do this like pros and do it in one take." Well, after the first take, which was not acceptable we did another and another. Finally, after six takes, we had a reasonably acceptable version of the appeal to young men. After several attempts with the message aimed at young women, we gave up, because it became obvious that his presentation to young women was not going to work.

Dr Harry Jonas, ACOG's incoming President had agreed to a meeting with Dr. John Wylie, the leader of the Right to Life movement to see, even though we disagreed on the issue of choice, if we could cooperate on a program to reduce unintended pregnancies which also would reduce the need for abortion in many cases. He asked me who he should take along to the meeting, and I advised him not to take anyone, because if he took an entourage, Wylie would do the same and it would turn into a meeting with everyone trying to emerge as the hero. My advice was to go solo and on his return to dictate what had transpired.

And that's what he did. He described a cordial meeting with Dr. Wylie saying he would like to cooperate on such a program, but he couldn't do it since that would split his movement which he described as having three parts: the small but violent group which he waved away. He then described the two major groups which were composed of those who say "No abortion but contraception is permissible" and those who say, "No abortion and no contraception." And with that, our effort to work together came to an end.

Iain Chalmers, whom I had met in Oxford during our stay in England, had established an organization called the Chochrane Group which collected the results from all controlled tests of health procedures making it possible to see what the collective wisdom said about any single procedure. Iain was going to be in Washington so I urged our medical directors to meet with him. They agreed with a little reluctance, but before the meeting was half over, it became evident that ACOG was going to become very interested in using this tool.

Shortly after the triumph with the networks, Laurie Hall left to have a baby so we advertised for a replacement. Terry Malone who worked in Dr. Harry Visscher's section at ACOG applied for the job. She seemed like a good candidate, so I offered her the job thereby creating a mild firestorm when Harry's people accused me of raiding their personnel. I had to remind them that Abraham Lincoln had freed the slaves. Before advertising for the press officer's job, I had negotiated with our personnel office (in the days before Human Resources) to have Florence and the press officer receive equal pay.

When the original three years of our campaign against unintended pregnancy was coming to an end, Dr. Ezra Davidson, who was the incoming president, called for the program to be extended for another three years. Without a dissenting voice, the board approved the extension.

There was one issue that haunted the members of ACOG of which I was aware from the moment I came on board and that was the problem of malpractice or, as they liked to call it "professional liability." I had resisted requests to address the issue in our Women's Health columns, because I wanted to keep the columns focused on providing useful information to the readers. Being a platform to advocate for an issue would, I believed, destroy the column's appeal.

Dr. Erv Nichols who headed the Practice Division of the college and his assistant, Elvoy Raines, grappled with the issue and what to do about it. I suggested that they conduct a survey of ACOG physicians, which had never been done, to get a national look at how the problem was affecting the profession.

I also took a careful look at the public's attitude toward physicians in general as opposed to attitudes toward "My Doctor" and found about what I expected. Using studies that had been conducted each year by the American Medical

Association (AMA), I found that the marks for personal physician were always greatly higher than for the profession as a whole. In other national surveys, doctors were rated fairly high and lawyers near the bottom.

We had developed a kit for ob/gyns allowing them to conduct studies of their patients' attitudes toward them and their practices. Although these surveys were not randomized and conducted from our physicians' own practices which meant that the results would tend to be more favorable than a survey of the general population, the results even when compared to the AMA studies, were revealing. We collected and tabulated data from 203 practices and almost 30,000 patients. Almost three out of every four were "very satisfied with the helpfulness of the physician and staff" with only about one quarter of the respondents finding fault with the running of the practices.

Taking these and other surveys into consideration, I began to question the obsession by our members with the malpractice problem. Of course, it was a shock each time a physician was sued, but was this obsession with the costs of malpractice insurance really justified. Then, I observed how this worked out in practice. Insurance costs amounted to about 10% of the doctor's gross, so when the insurance companies in Florida raised the premiums by 10% one year, the Florida ob/gyns raised their fees 10%. The next year, premiums were reduced.

At a committee meeting to discuss ways to address the malpractice insurance problem, I used this as an example first telling the committee that we had raised public awareness of the problem. Then I pointed to the Florida example and asked, "How many doctors reduced their fees the next year when the insurance companies reduced the premiums?" I asked the question and was greeted with a profound silence.

Three doctors at Washington's Women's Hospital had recently lost a malpractice suit and had been approached by Mike Wallace for an interview on "60 Minutes." They asked me for some advice on how to handle the request. I urged them to accept the interview since I had heard that Wallace wasn't particularly fond of lawyers. In preparing them for the interview, they told me why they had lost the suit. Since they knew they had done everything right in spite of the bad outcome, they had come across as arrogant on the witness stand. The prosecuting lawyer was also very good, better than theirs, and the damaged baby was in the courtroom. The interview went well, but probably didn't change anyone's minds.

At meeting after meeting, I urged the doctors, when being interviewed by the media not to dwell on attacking attorneys. I pointed to numerous studies that showed public approval of attorneys was extremely low. They, the doctors, didn't have to attack the lawyers; the public already had. I would show our doctors a video clip of a Florida doctor in a very well appointed office wearing a multi-hundred dollar suit saying, "The only ones making money off this are a small group of very wealthy lawyers." When I asked our doctors for reaction to this video, none of them could spot the silliness of this obviously well to do doctor complaining about well to do lawyers.

During this period, Eileen embarked on her third career; this time as an author and historian. Her first book was published by the Smithsonian Press was *Cal Rodgers and the Vin Fiz* the story of the first flight across the country in 1911. It received very good reviews including one in the *New York*

Times which wrote "Lebow's account is a wonderful window on America before the communication era." Another reviewer wrote that "Books about the earliest days of aviation are, with rare exceptions, boring to all but the most dedicated and enthusiastic aviation historians. A notable exception is *Cal Rodgers and the Vin Fiz: the first Transcontinental Flight*. The book is fun as well as educational." She would eventually have six books with her byline. Her work habits put me to shame. She would spend two to three hours at either the Library of Congress or the National Archives, come home for lunch and to read the newspaper, then two to three hours at her computer typing out her text.

    About this time, Terry Malone left to be married, and Kate Ruddon, who was working as an information officer at the National Cancer Institute saw the advertisement for the vacancy and applied. She turned out to be a jewel for the job. She required practically no direct supervision, and in a very short time, she was handling requests from reporters covering our beat with a professionalism that couldn't be beat. We lucked out.

On November 2, 1989, *the New England Journal of Medicine* published a study of Swedish women's use of estrogen replacement therapy and the risk of breast cancer. The study of the prescription records of 23,244 women who had estrogen replacement therapies concluded that long term use of these therapies were associated with a slightly increased risk of breast cancer. The ensuing publicity generated a panic, not only among women but also with a number of doctors who began to question their own treatment of their patients.

Gina Kolata, a correspondent for the *New York Times*, excitedly called demanding, "What are you going to do about this?" After pointing out that the study showed that the estrogen used by American women actually showed a decreased risk although it was from a very small sample, she went ahead and wrote what I expected from her--that this large study of Swedish women showed that women who used estrogen replacement therapy risked getting cancer of the breast. It was only when you read down through the middle of the second column that a reader could find the reassuring words that "Most of the women in the Swedish study took a different formulation of estrogen than Americans take."

The story exploded from there with newspapers and TV shows across the country stoking the fears and even aided by the press release from the National Cancer Institute which failed to mention the non-American estrogen that was used. Few major newspapers treated the story in a balanced fashion except the one written by Jim Friend of *USA Today*.

It was left for us, the organization representing the 29,000 physicians who were prescribing these therapies to issue statements trying to give a balanced view, but our statements and releases, of course, could be viewed as self-serving and less believable. Although the tempest passed after awhile, I was bothered by how the otherwise respectable media had latched on to the more lurid details of the story without any of the balancing reassurances that were part of the study. So, with Kate handling press inquiries so well, and Florence running the office so handily, I occasionally would visit the periodical room of the Library of Congress working on a study that would take me into my retirement.

At my annual performance review, Warren told me to put in my budget money for another staff member if I needed it. I declined saying that with Florence and Kate, we had enough to handle our work without getting in each other's way. I thought it was nice of him to make the offer but didn't know how this would shortly affect our work.

It was sometime after this that I was visited by Richard Huttner and Susan Strecker the editors of *Baby Talk* magazine with a proposal for a new periodical called *Baby on the Way*. Dick wanted ACOG's endorsement for the project. I explained that we did not give endorsements. Dick quickly accepted my offer to have our doctors produce by-lined articles that were written by us and their staff and cleared by ACOG. Everything I proposed, which I thought might end the conversation, only met with agreement. So, with the possibility of ACOG physicians having a magazine vetted by us and available for their patients, I arranged for Dick to make his presentation to Warren.

Since, by all rights, this project should very well be handled by Dr. Harry Visscher and his staff, he was invited to attend the presentation. After Dick gave his spiel and left to await our verdict,

Warren asked Harry if he could handle this with his present staff. When Harry, as expected, said he could not do it without more staff, Warren turned to me, and I volunteered that we could handle it thinking of our conversation during my last performance review. So it was set: *Baby on the Way* would be published by the staff of *Baby Talk* magazine as an ACOG publication.

Working with Susan, Kate and I wrote and vetted articles for the magazine, and Florence would handle, as she always did so well, all the details of meeting the requests from our physicians for distribution to their patients. It wasn't until the first issue made its appearance when I was sitting with Kate and admiring the magazine that I thought back to the literacy material we had produced at Social Security for the Migrant Ministry and wondered if we could turn out a magazine like this but one aimed at people who could not read at more than a grade school level." It was from that thought that we were going to embark on a very rewarding path.

After developing a proposal that was based on a three legged approach, I discussed it with Dick Huttner. My proposal was that ACOG, with the expertise of an organization like the Literacy Volunteers of America (LVA) and the publishing and advertising backup of the *Baby Talk* organization would produce and distribute a publication *Baby on the Way: Basics* aimed at the low literacy market of expectant parents.

I was unprepared for the negative reaction from Huttner. Thinking, erroneously I believe, there was no advertising market for such a magazine, he was unenthusiastic and priced his participation at an outrageously high level. At the same time, he proudly announced a new project for another magazine aimed at expectant mothers.

Not willing to give up on a basic magazine, I considered pitching my idea to another publisher. I took out the contract we had signed with *Baby Talk* and found that neither of us could produce any other magazine without permission from the other party. So ACOG was bound to *Baby Talk*, and they were bound to us. Not feeling any shame about how I was going to spoil Dick's New Year's celebration, I phoned to tell him that he was breaking his contract with us by going ahead with his new publication without our permission. He was dumbfounded, and after I pointed out the part of the contract that bound us together, he said he would get back to me.

It was after New Years that he came down to Washington and admitted that I had ruined his New Year's celebration. He also, with more confidence than was justified, proudly presented me with an offer of royalties to ACOG in exchange for permission to go forward with his new magazine. I turned him down and then told him that if he would make it easy for us to produce *Baby on_the Way: Basics*, I would make it easy for him to go ahead with his magazine feeling no guilt whatsoever at my blackmail effort. A few days later, he came back with a much reduced cost for producing the literacy effort. Between contributions from the Pew Charitable Trust, Carnation Nutritional Products and the ACOG Development Fund, we were on our way.

After contacting the LVA, Susan Strecker and I visited them at their national headquarters in Syracuse. At first, I detected a suspicion on their part of this request from a doctor's organization and a publishing outfit to work with them to produce this new product, but after explaining how we had come up with the idea for this new magazine aimed at a very elusive audience and how we would cover all their costs, they agreed to be our partners in the venture.

As Kate and I at ACOG and Susan at *Baby Talk* prepared articles for the new magazine, I scheduled a meeting with the staff of the Women, Infant and Children (WIC) program at the US Department of Agriculture to enlist their support in distributing copies to their clients who were low income women who I thought could benefit from our effort. Once again, I was met with skepticism by a staff that viewed this as another way to increase business for our doctors. Luckily, the director of the WIC program didn't share the view of much of his staff and agreed to help.

With all the articles finished and checked for accuracy, the LVA gave us guidance to make sure the articles were written at a grade school level and convened some focus groups to see how the articles would fare with the targeted audiences. Then we were ready to go to press completely unprepared for the avalanche that was about to descend on us.

When an initial print run of 250,000 proved completely inadequate, we ultimately raised the number to 600,000 and even then had to limit distribution to 100 copies to each physician's office and 250 for each clinic, practice or literacy program. Even with these limits, the demand quickly outran our supply. The PHS asked for 160,000 for their Healthy Start program sites. We mailed a one page promotion with an order form to 1,700 WIC programs, 1,300 Maternal and Child Health programs, 4,500 literacy programs and 31,000 Fellows of ACOG. In spite of our stated limits, many state agencies requested copies far in excess with the Arizona WIC program asking for 10,000 copies and the Mississippi Health Department asking for 15,000. In all, we received almost 6,000 requests for more than one million copies.

And then, one day Florence, who had been handling the flood of requests, received a phone call from the editors of the *Library Journal* to let her know that *Baby on the Way: Basics* had been selected as one of the ten best magazines of the year. When she didn't reply with the expected elation, the editor seemed surprised until Florence explained how inundated we were with requests for the magazine.

It was shortly after this, after consulting with Eileen, during my annual performance review that I told Warren that I was giving him a year's notice that I was going to retire. He was quite surprised and asked, "What are we going to do?" And I calmly answered, "You're going to hire someone else." I agreed to help select candidates for my replacement. With the benefit of hindsight, I probably should have hung on for another couple of years and groomed Kate for the job.

After a splendid farewell party arranged by Florence, I was on my way out the door, although I still had a tenuous role for two years in promoting *Baby on the Way: Basics*. It was two years later that ACOG gave me a distinguished service award, the first time that a non-doctor was so honored.

Forty years before, it had all started when I had first met and saw George Richards, a civil servant, who made it his business to make the people he served feel very important.

Chapter Twelve
1998-1999

I also had one lingering thought of something I wanted to finish. Watching the alarmist news stories about the bad effects of the contraceptive pill which was at variance with the scientific evidence, I decided to do a study of how newspapers covered the scientific studies being published in the journals. This was going to have me spending a great deal of time in the periodical room of the Library of Congress.

Using Medline, I identified the nine major studies on the health effects of oral contraception (OC) that were published 1986 through 1997 in the two major medical journals in the US: *The New England Journal of Medicine* and *The Journal of the American Medical Association*. I then looked at how four major newspapers: The *New York Times*, *The Washington Post*, *The Chicago Tribune* and the *Los Angeles Times,* reported these studies on the health effects of OC and found some surprising and discouraging results.

Of the nine stories in *the New England Journal and JAMA* on the health effects of OC, which found either no increased risks or protective effects, only one study was covered by all four papers. That study in the *New England Journal* in August 1986, received prominent coverage in three of the four papers, the *NY Times* was the exception placing the story on a back page. Five studies, including one that found the OC protected against endometrial cancer and another that found protection against ovarian cancer, were not reported by any of the papers. Two other studies, one that reported no increased risk of breast cancer and the other that found no increased risk of coronary heart disease, received minor coverage, each by a single paper. The fifth study, which demonstrated that proper dosage of OC protects against coronary heart disease, received negative treatment in the *Washington Post*, the one paper that reported the study.

After completing the manuscript of my findings, I sent to it Dr. Roy Pitkin, the editor of the journal *Obstetrics & Gynecology* Dr. Pitkin, where it appeared on March, 1999. And that was that as I slid contentedly into full retirement.

Printed in Great Britain
by Amazon